Windows® 95
The Visual Learning Guide

Other Prima Visual Learning Guides

Word for Windows 95: The Visual Learning Guide
Excel for Windows 95: The Visual Learning Guide
WinComm PRO: The Visual Learning Guide
PROCOMM PLUS for Windows: The Visual Learning Guide
WordPerfect 6.1 for Windows: The Visual Learning Guide
Word 6 for the Mac: The Visual Learning Guide
Cruising America Online
Quicken for Windows: The Visual Learning Guide
1-2-3 for Windows: The Visual Learning Guide
ACT! 2.0 for Windows: The Visual Learning Guide
Excel for the Mac: The Visual Learning Guide
Windows 3.1: The Visual Learning Guide
Excel 5 for Windows: The Visual Learning Guide
PowerPoint: The Visual Learning Guide
Word for Windows 6: The Visual Learning Guide
WordPerfect 6 for Windows: The Visual Learning Guide
WinFax PRO: The Visual Learning Guide

Upcoming Books!

Sidekick: The Visual Learning Guide
Internet for Windows America Online 2.5 Edition
Access for Windows 95: The Visual Learning Guide
PowerPoint for Windows 95: The Visual Learning Guide

How to Order:
Individual orders and quantity discounts are available from the publisher, Prima Publishing, P.O. Box 1260BK, Rocklin, CA 95677-1260; (916) 632-4400. For quantity orders, include information on your letterhead concerning the intended use of the books and the number of books you wish to purchase.

Windows® 95

The Visual Learning Guide

Grace Joely Beatty, Ph.D.

David C. Gardner, Ph.D.

PRIMA PUBLISHING

Project Editor: Susan Silva

If you have problems installing or running Windows® 95 contact Microsoft at (206) 882-8080. Prima Publishing cannot provide software support.

Prima Publishing and the authors have attempted throughout this book to distinguish proprietary trademarks from descriptive terms by following the capitalization style used by the manufacturer.

Information contained in this book has been obtained by Prima Publishing from sources believed to be reliable. However, because of the possibility of human or mechanical error by our sources, Prima Publishing, or others, the Publisher does not guarantee the accuracy, adequacy, or completeness of any information and is not responsible for any errors or omissions or the results obtained from use of such information.

ISBN: 1-55958-738-5
Library of Congress Catalog Card Number: 94-68667
97 98 AA 10 9 8 7 6 5 4
Printed in the United States of America

Acknowledgments

We are deeply indebted to reviewers around the country who gave so generously of their time to test every step in the manuscript. David Coburn, Moshen Fallahi, Carolyn Holder, Ray Holder, Ellen Lewis, Joshua Nye, David Sauer, Catherine M. Sullivan, Tina Terhark, and Mark C. Turner cannot be thanked enough! In addition to manuscript testing, David Sauer and Carolyn Holder added their magic touch to the Installation chapter.

We are personally and professionally delighted to work with everyone at Prima Publishing.

Linda Miles, technical editor; Becky Whitney, copy editor; Marian Hartsough, layout; Katherine Stimson, indexer; and Paul Page, cover design, contributed immensely to the final product.

Bill Gladstone and Matt Wagner of Waterside Productions created the idea for this series. Their faith in us has never wavered.

Joseph and Shirley Beatty made this series possible. We can never repay them.

Asher Shapiro has always been there when we needed him.

Paula Gardner Capaldo and David Capaldo have been terrific. Thanks, Joshua and Jessica, for being such wonderful kids!

We could not have met the deadlines without the technical support of Ray Holder, our electrical genius, Diana M. Balelo, Frank E. Straw, Daniel W. Terhark and Martin J. O'Keefe of Computer Service & Maintenance, our computer wizards. Thank you all! Daniel Terhark especially went above and beyond the call of duty, helping us navigate the rough waters of system conversion, network restructuring, and capturing installation screens. Dan, you're a genius as well as a great guy!

Contents at a Glance

Customize Your Learning

Prima Visual Learning Guides™ are not like any other computer books you have ever seen. They are based on our years in the classroom, our corporate consulting, and our research at Boston University on the best ways to teach technical information to non-technical learners. Most importantly, this series is based on the feedback of a panel of reviewers from across the country who range in computer knowledge from "panicked at the thought" to sophisticated.

Each chapter is illustrated with color screens to guide you through every task. The combination of screens, step-by-step instructions, and pointers makes it impossible for you to get lost or confused as you follow along on your own computer.

LET US KNOW . . .

We truly hope that you'll like using this book and Windows® 95. Let us know how you feel about our book and whether there are any changes or improvements we can make. You can contact us through Prima Publishing or send us an e-mail letter. Our Internet address is write.bks@aol.com.

Thanks for buying the book. Have fun!

Joely and David

WINDOWS 95

Part I: Getting Acquainted with Windows 95

Starting Windows 95 and Opening a Program

If you've never used Windows before, you'll be amazed at how easy it is to learn. If you've used Windows 3.1, you'll find that the transition to 95 is like going to a newer, fancier car. It still does the same things; it just does them faster. And, of course, it has newer, fancier buttons and gadgets that give it exciting new capabilities. In this chapter, you will do the following:

✔ Start Windows 95

✔ Open one of the programs that comes with Windows 95

STARTING WINDOWS 95

When you start your computer, you'll hear some "computer-at-work" humming and crunching noises as your computer "boots up" Windows 95. Boot up is a computer term that means start, or open.

How quickly Windows 95 starts depends on the speed of your computer. After a short time, you'll see the Windows 95 logo you see here. Continue to let Windows do its thing and eventually you'll see the screen shown on the next page.

WELCOME TO WINDOWS

Every time you open Windows 95, you'll see the Welcome screen and a "Did you know..." tip.

1. If you want to take the Windows tour, **click** on the **Windows Tour button** and follow the directions on your screen. You don't have to take it now, however. You can take the Windows tour at any time by clicking on this button. If you installed Windows 95 as an upgrade over Windows 3.1, you may not have this button.

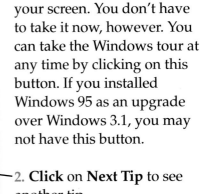

2. **Click** on **Next Tip** to see another tip.

3. **Click** on **Close** to close Welcome to Windows.

When you become familiar with Windows, you may not want to see the Welcome window each time you turn on your computer. See Chapter 10 for directions on turning off the Tip of the Day.

THE OPENING SCREEN

Windows 95 allows for tremendous customization. Your screen may not look exactly like the one in this example. You may see one or more of the following icons, or pictures:

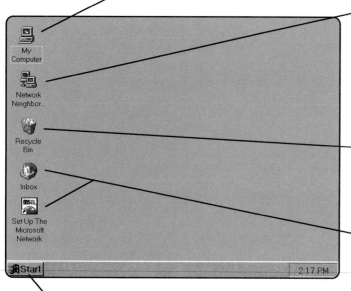

❖ **My Computer** contains details about how your computer is set up. You'll learn how to use this feature in Chapters 10, 16, and 18.

❖ **Network Neighborhood** means that your computer is connected to a network. If you bought your computer for home use, you probably don't have this icon.

❖ **Recycle Bin** is used to delete files. You'll learn how it works in Chapter 18.

The **Inbox** and **Set Up The Microsoft Network** are part of Microsoft's Exchange program, which is a separately purchased program. These are covered in depth in our book *Internet for Windows, Microsoft Network Edition*. If you don't want to buy Microsoft Exchange, you can delete these icons from your desktop. See Chapter 10 for details. We won't show these icons in the rest of the examples in this book.

Depending on how your computer was set up, you may see icons not shown here.

❖ In the next section, you'll use the Start button on the **taskbar** to open a program that comes with Windows 95.

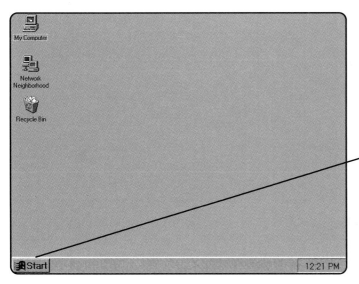

USING THE START BUTTON

The Start button is one of the ways to get at what is on your computer.

1. **Move** your **mouse** until the mouse arrow is on top of the Start button on the taskbar.

2. **Click** the **left mouse button**. A pop-up *menu*, or list of choices, will appear.

Take a moment to look at the pop-up menu. You'll learn how to use each of the options listed on the menu as you go through this book.

Notice that the top four options have a ▶ to the right. You'll learn the significance of the ▶ in the next step.

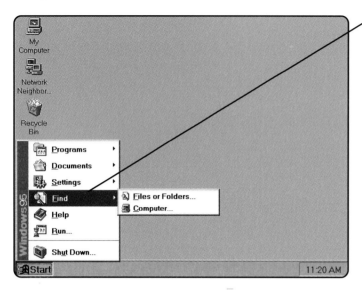

3. Move the mouse arrow up to Find. A highlight bar will move as you move the mouse arrow. Let your mouse arrow (and the highlight bar) rest on Find.

Another menu will appear to the side. The ▶ to the right of Find means that another menu will appear when you highlight this choice. "Computer" will be on the second menu only if you're on a network.

In this example, you will ignore the Find menu and move up to Programs.

4. Move the mouse arrow up to **Programs**. The high-light bar will move as you move the mouse arrow. Depending on how fast or slow you move your mouse, additional pop-up menus may appear as you drag the highlight bar up the menu. Just ignore them.

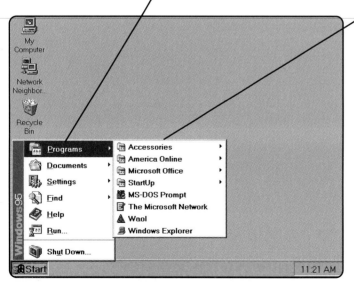

When you highlight Programs, another pop-up menu will appear. Notice that this new menu also has items that have a ▶ to the right. As you now know, each ▶ means that another menu will appear.

Depending on how your computer is set up, you may see items on the menu that are different from the ones you see here.

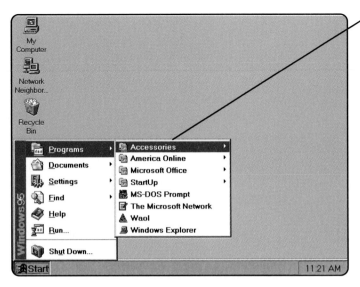

5. **Slide** the mouse arrow over to **Accessories** to highlight it. A new pop-up menu will appear. It may appear in a different place from the one in the next example.

Notice that several options on the new menu have a ▶ to the right.

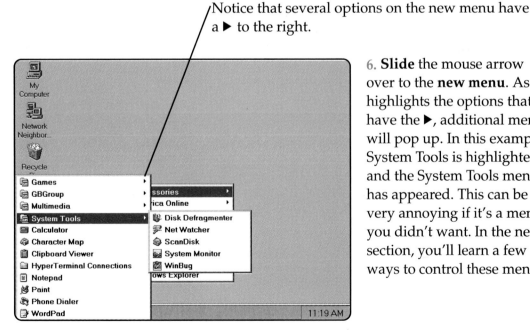

6. **Slide** the mouse arrow over to the **new menu**. As it highlights the options that have the ▶, additional menus will pop up. In this example, System Tools is highlighted and the System Tools menu has appeared. This can be very annoying if it's a menu you didn't want. In the next section, you'll learn a few ways to control these menus.

Controlling Pop-Up Menus

The pop-up menus can get a little hyperactive and pop up all over the place. There are several ways to control them.

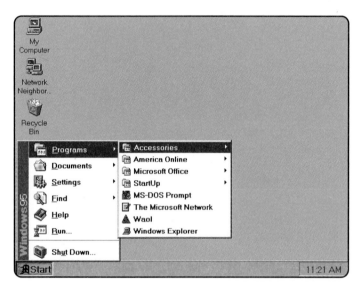

1. **Press** the **Esc key** on your keyboard. You will go back one pop-up menu. Continue to press the Esc key to remove additional levels. (Sometimes your computer doesn't believe that you want to go back one level, and the pop-up menu will pop right back up. Be firm and press the Esc key a second time.)

2. **Press** the **Esc key** until you are back at the screen you see below.

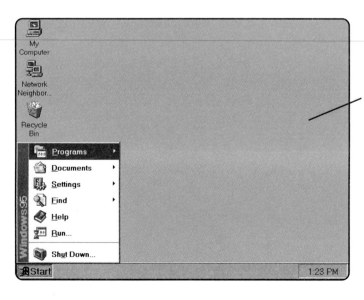

A second way to get rid of uncontrollable pop-up menus is to start all over again.

3. **Move** the mouse arrow to **any clear space** on your screen.

4. **Click** the **left mouse button**. All open menus will close and you'll have a clear screen.

OPENING A PROGRAM

Now that you've had some experience using the pop-up menus, you're ready to open WordPad, one of the programs that comes with Windows 95. All programs in Windows 95 can be opened in the same way.

1. Click on the **Start button** on the taskbar. A pop-up menu will appear.

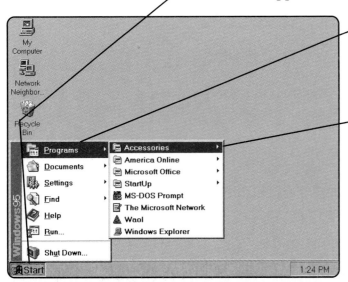

2. Move the mouse arrow **up** the menu to highlight **Programs**. A second menu will appear.

3. Move the mouse arrow over to **Accessories**. A third menu will appear.

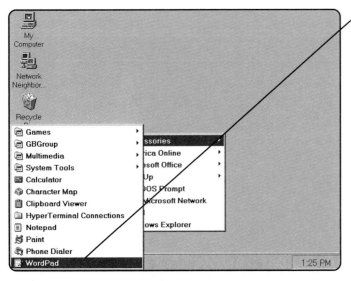

4. Move the mouse arrow **down** to **WordPad**. Notice that this option doesn't have a ▶ to the right. When you highlight it, nothing happens until you do step 5.

5. Click the **left mouse button**. This will open WordPad.

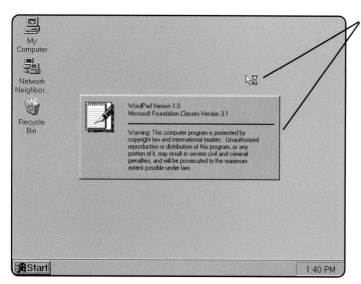

You'll see an hourglass and then the message window you see in this example. In a very short time, you'll see the WordPad window shown below.

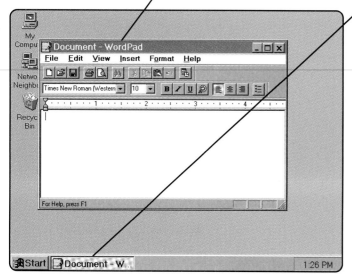

This is the opening screen in WordPad, a word-processing program that comes with Windows 95. It may appear in a different spot and be a different size from what you see here.

Notice that a button for WordPad also appears on the taskbar.

WordPad is great for writing simple letters or memos. You'll learn how to use it in Chapter 12, "Writing a Memo in WordPad." Right now, you'll use WordPad to learn how to change the size and position of a window. Go on to Chapter 2 for step-by-step directions.

Changing the Size and Position of a Window

You have tremendous control over how things look on your screen when you work in Windows. In this chapter, you will do the following:

✔ Use the Maximize button to enlarge a window

✔ Use the Restore button to return a window to its initial size

✔ Manually enlarge a window

✔ Move a window

✔ Minimize a program

ENLARGING A WINDOW

When you work in a program such as WordPad, it's very helpful to have as much working area as possible. Windows has a special button that lets you maximize the size of a window at the click of your mouse.

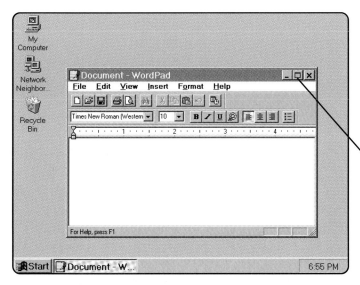

If you've been following along with this book, you have WordPad open on your screen. If not, go back to Chapter 1 to learn how to open WordPad.

1. **Click** on the **Maximize button** (□) on the right side of the WordPad title bar. The WordPad window will fill the screen.

RESTORING A WINDOW TO ITS INITIAL SIZE

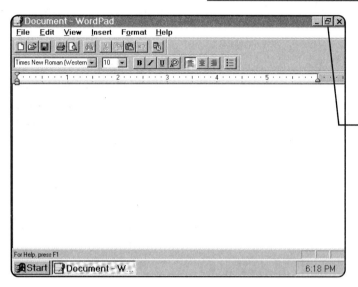

After you maximize a window, the Maximize button (□) changes shape and becomes the Restore button (🗗).

1. **Click** on the **Restore button** (🗗) on the right of the WordPad title bar. The WordPad window will be returned to its initial size.

In the next section, you'll learn another way to increase the size of a window.

MANUALLY ENLARGING A WINDOW

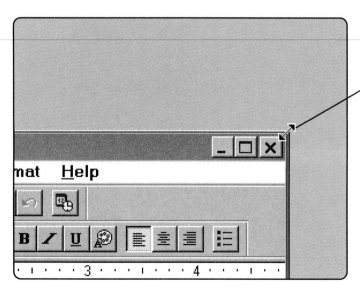

You can use your mouse to give your window a specific shape.

1. **Place** the mouse arrow on the **upper right corner** of the window. The mouse will change shape to the two-headed arrow you see here. You may have to fiddle with the position of the mouse arrow to get it to change shape. This is, by the way, a close-up view of the upper right corner of your screen.

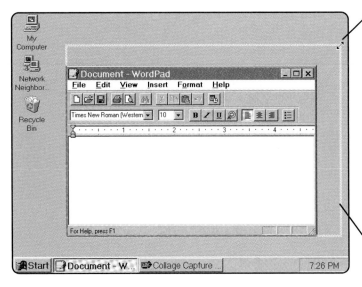

2. Press and hold the **left mouse button** and **drag** the **corner** of the window up **toward** the **right corner** of the screen. You'll see an outline of the window expand as you drag the two-headed arrow. You can adjust the size of the outline as long as you continue to hold down the mouse button.

3. Release the mouse button when the outline is about the size of the one you see here. The window will become the size of the outline.

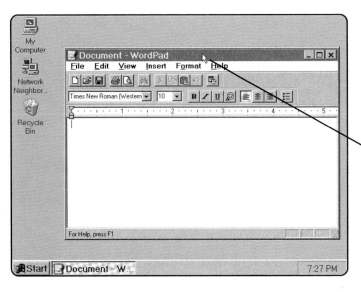

MOVING A WINDOW

You can move any window that has a title bar.

1. Place the mouse arrow on **top** of the WordPad **title bar**.

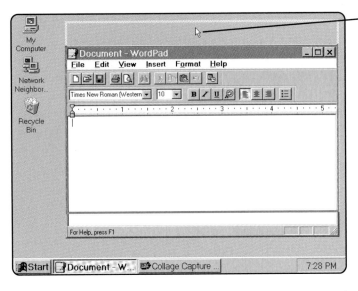

2. Press and hold the **left mouse button** and drag the window **toward** the **top** of the screen. You'll see an outline of the window being moved as you drag the mouse arrow. You can continue to fiddle with the placement of the window as long as you hold down the mouse button.

3. Release the mouse button when the window is about where you see here. The window will stay in this spot until you change it.

Now when you click on the Maximize button and then on the Restore button, the window will be restored to this new size. Try it for yourself.

MINIMIZING A PROGRAM

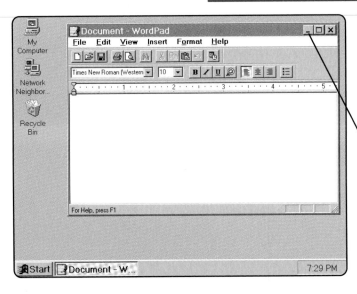

When you minimize a program, you actually make it run in the background. It is not visible on your screen but is only a mouse click away.

1. Click on the **Minimize button** (☐) on the right side of the WordPad title bar. The program will disappear into the taskbar at the bottom of your screen.

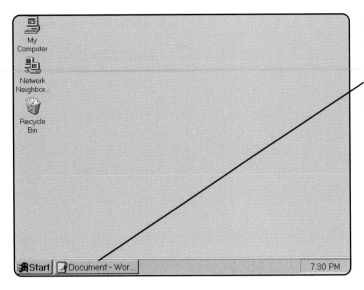

USING THE TASKBAR

Notice that when a program is minimized, it seems to disappear into the taskbar. It is actually running in your computer's memory, and you can use the taskbar to bring it up at any time.

The taskbar has another feature, called balloons, that tells you about each item on the taskbar.

1. **Place** the mouse arrow on **top** of the **Document button**. Notice that the button isn't big enough to show the full name of the program. Let the mouse rest on the button for a few seconds.

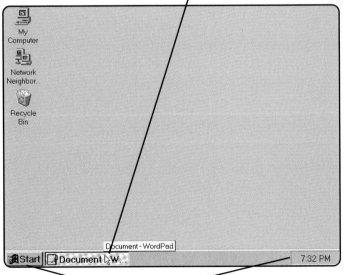

Notice the balloon that pops up to tell you what this button represents. The balloon tells you the full name of the program. You may have to fiddle with the placement of the arrow to get the balloon.

2. **Repeat step 1** for the Start button and the time button.

In the next chapter, you'll learn how to have several programs open at the same time.

Switching Between Open Programs

If you're just getting used to using a computer, you may wonder why you would want to have more than one program open at the same time. Think of it as having multiple file folders on your desk and being able to go back and forth between them for information. In this chapter, you will do the following:

✔ Open the calculator on top of WordPad

✔ Switch between programs

BRINGING AN OPEN PROGRAM TO THE FOREGROUND

In Chapter 2 you minimized WordPad into the taskbar. Even though you cannot see WordPad, it is open and "running in the background," as they say in Windows lingo. In this example, you'll use the button on the taskbar to bring it "to the foreground" again.

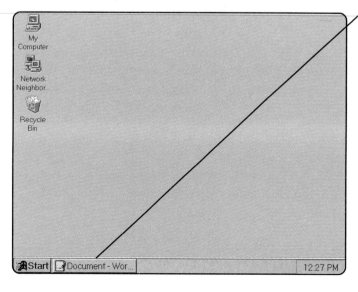

1. **Place** the mouse arrow on **top** of the **WordPad button** and **click** the **left mouse button**. WordPad will be returned to your screen.

Note: If you're new to Windows, we hope you're getting used to the idea of moving the mouse arrow to an item, and then clicking the left mouse button to open the program. From here, we'll shorten it to just "click on whatever."

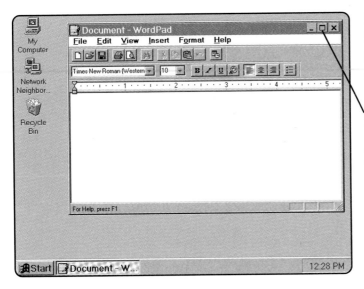

Notice that WordPad appears in the same size and position it was in the last time it was on your screen.

2. Click on the **Maximize button** (□) on the right side of the title bar to make WordPad fill the screen.

STARTING A SECOND PROGRAM

In this section, you have WordPad on your screen. Let's pretend that you're typing a quick memo and you discover that you need to add some numbers so that you can put a "total" figure in your memo. You can rummage around in your desk for a calculator, or you can open the one that comes with Windows. You can open the calculator even though WordPad is on your screen.

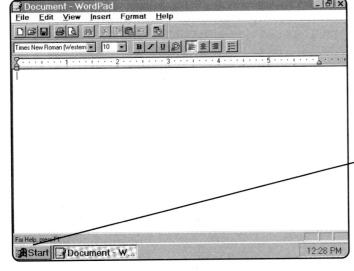

1. Click on the **Start button** on the taskbar. A pop-up menu will appear.

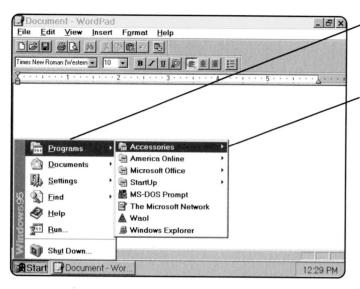

2. **Move** the mouse arrow up to **Programs**. A pop-up menu will appear.

3. **Move** the mouse arrow over to **Accessories**. Another menu will appear.

4. **Move** the mouse arrow to **Calculator**.

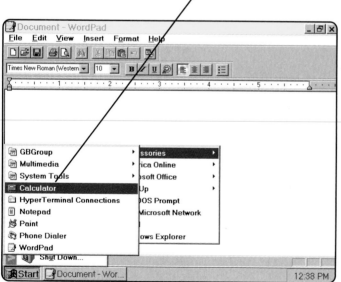

5. **Press** the **Enter key** on your keyboard. The calculator will appear on your screen. (Pressing Enter does the same thing as clicking on the highlighted choice.)

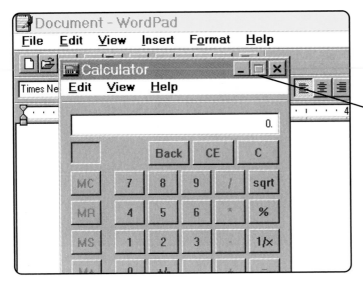

Trying to Use an Unavailable Function

1. Click on the grayed-out **Maximize button**. Notice that *nothing happens*.

The fact that the Maximize button is grayed out means that you cannot maximize the calculator. This is as big as it gets. When a function is not available, it is grayed out.

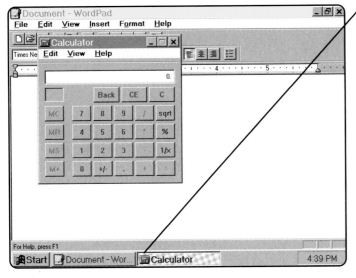

Notice that the Calculator button on the taskbar appears pressed in. This means that the calculator is the "active program." If you try to type words, nothing happens because the calculator is not set up to accept words. Try typing a few letters. (Nothing happens, right?) You have to make WordPad the "active" program in order to use it.

In the next section, you'll learn one way to do that.

SENDING THE CALCULATOR TO THE BACKGROUND

As you use Windows, you'll learn that there are several ways to do the same thing. In this example, you'll send the calculator to the background and bring WordPad to the foreground. Because you can see WordPad behind the calculator, there's a really easy way to do it.

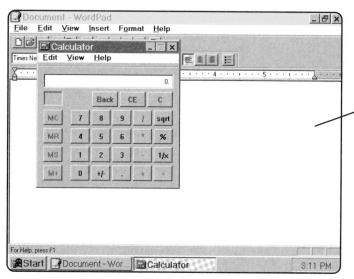

1. **Click anywhere** on the WordPad screen. The calculator will disappear from view, and WordPad will be the only program on your screen.

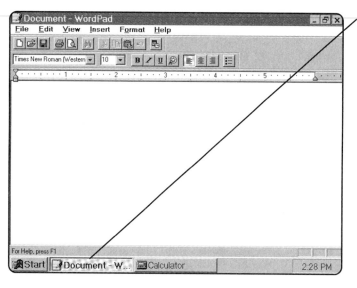

Notice that the WordPad button on the taskbar now looks pressed in and is lighter in color than the calculator button. This tells you that WordPad is now the active program.

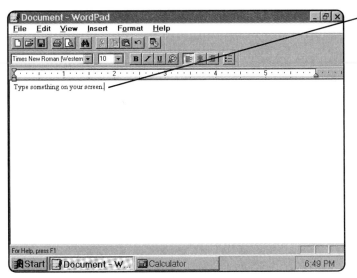

2. Type the **sentence** below. There will be a brief pause between the time you start typing and the time you see the words appear on your screen.

Type something on your screen.

SWITCHING TO THE CALCULATOR

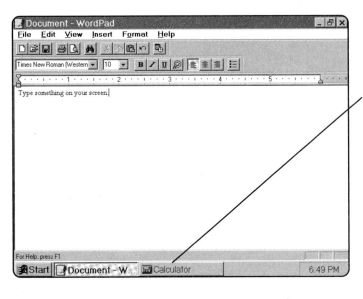

Even when you have text on the screen, you can switch to another open program.

1. Click on the **Calculator button** on the taskbar. The calculator will appear on your screen.

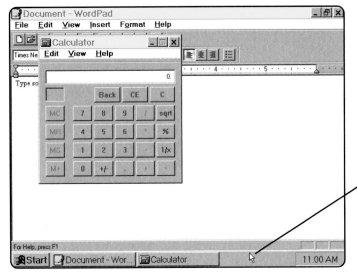

PUTTING PROGRAMS SIDE BY SIDE

Windows has a feature called *tiling* that will put programs side by side on your screen.

1. **Move** the mouse arrow **down into** the **taskbar**, as you see in this example.

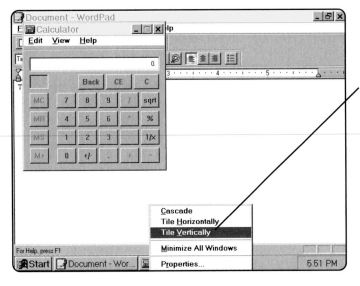

2. **Click** the **right mouse button**. A pop-up menu will appear.

3. **Click** on **Tile Vertically**. WordPad and the calculator (the two programs currently open) will appear side by side. (If you had clicked on Tile Horizontally, the programs would appear with one above the other.)

Switching Between Active Windows

When you have more than one window on your screen, only one can be active at a time. You make a window active by clicking on it.

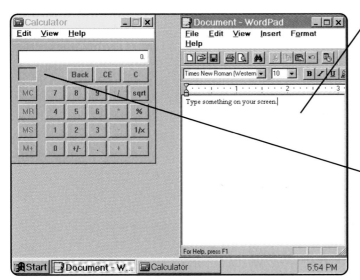

1. **Click anywhere** on the WordPad window. Notice that the title bar changes color. The color of the active title bar can be customized. See Chapter 5, "Customizing Colors."

2. **Click** on the **calculator** (but not on one of the keys). The title bar on the calculator will change color.

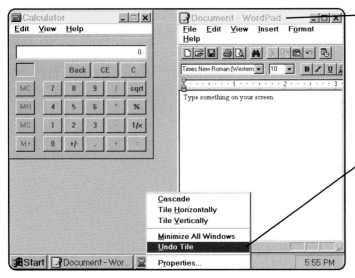

3. **Click** on the **WordPad** window once more.

4. **Move** the mouse arrow to the **taskbar** and **click** the *right* **mouse button**. A pop-up menu will appear.

5. **Click** on **Undo Tile**. The programs will be untiled, and the active program (in this case, WordPad) will be on your screen.

CLOSING PROGRAMS

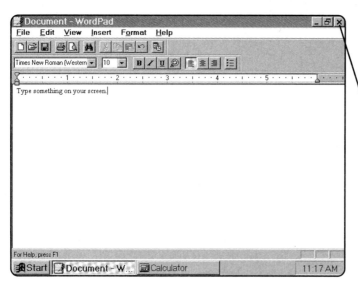

In this example, you'll close WordPad without saving the sentence you typed.

1. **Click** on the **Close button** ([X]) on the right side of the WordPad title bar.

Windows knows that you typed something into WordPad, and it won't let you close the program without giving you the option of saving the material.

In this example, you won't save the sentence you typed in WordPad. Remember, you can learn about WordPad in detail in Chapter 12, "Writing a Memo in WordPad."

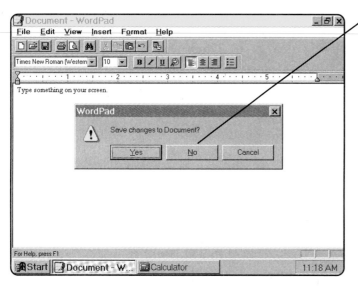

2. **Click** on **No**. WordPad will close, and its button will disappear from the taskbar. The calculator will still be on your screen.

In this example, you'll close the calculator. (It works just like a regular calculator, by the way. Just click on the appropriate key to enter numbers.) You'll learn more about the Calculator feature in Chapter 14, "Exploring the Three C's."

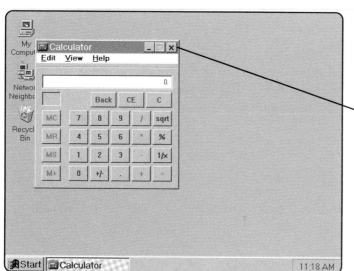

3. Click on the **Close button** ([X]) on the right side of the calculator title bar. The calculator will close, and its button will be removed from the taskbar. You'll be back at the desktop.

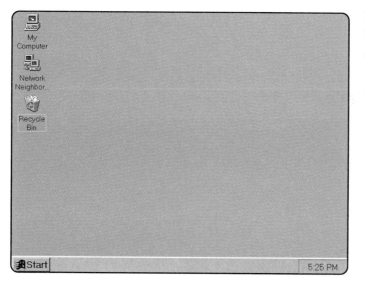

In the next chapter, you'll learn the right way to shut down your computer.

Shutting Down Your Computer

Be sure to close any open programs before you shut down your computer. This will allow you to save any work you've been doing that you forgot to save. It will also prevent any damage to your files. In this chapter, you will do the following:

✔ Shut down your computer

✔ Restart your computer

Note: If you don't want to shut your computer down right now, come back to this chapter when you're ready.

SHUTTING DOWN YOUR COMPUTER

Windows 95 conveniently includes a special option to shut itself off.

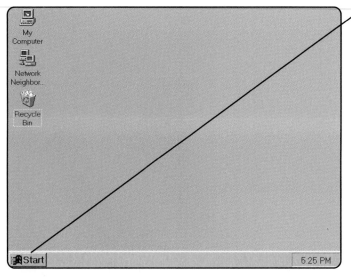

1. Click on the **Start button** on the taskbar. A pop-up menu will appear.

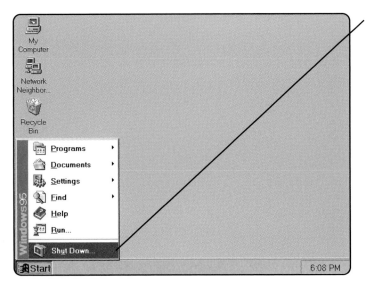

2. **Click** on **Shut Down**. The Shut Down Windows dialog box will appear.

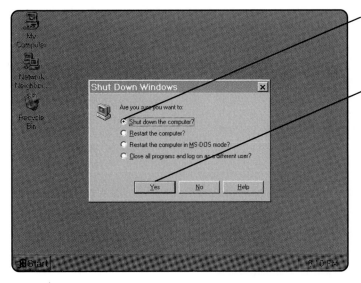

3. **Confirm** that **Shut down the computer?** has a dot in the circle.

4. **Click** on **Yes**. After a brief pause, you'll see the screen in the next example.

You'll see this screen. After a brief wait, you'll see the screen below.

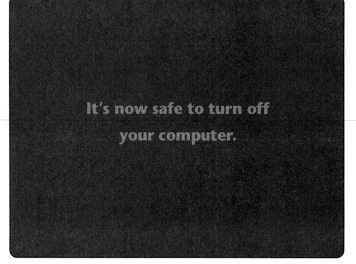

You can now turn off your computer.

If you want to continue with some of the chapters in this book, start your computer again.

WINDOWS 95

Part II: Customizing Windows

Customizing Colors

The colors you see in Windows screens can be customized. In this chapter, you will do the following:

✔ Choose from a number of predesigned color schemes
✔ Create your own color scheme

OPENING THE CONTROL PANEL

Before you can begin to customize the colors and patterns on your screen, you'll need to open the Control Panel window.

1. Click on the **Start button** on the taskbar. A pop-up menu will appear.

2. Move the mouse arrow to **Settings**. A second menu will appear.

3. Click on **Control Panel**. The Control Panel window will appear.

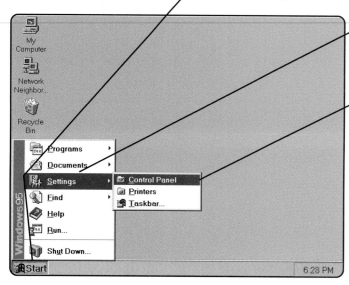

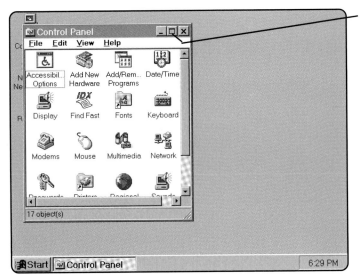

4. **Click** on the **Maximize button** (☐) on the right side of the Control Panel title bar to make the Control Panel window fill your screen. The icons may be arranged differently from those in the example below.

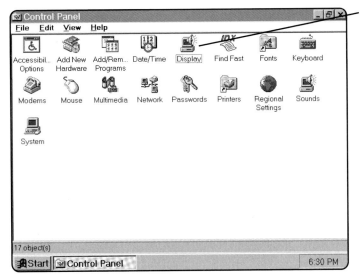

5. **Click twice** on the **Display icon**. It may be in a different spot on your screen. You'll see an hourglass, and then the Display Properties window will appear.

Note: If nothing happens when you click twice, try again. Place the mouse arrow on top of the Display icon. Hold the mouse steady and click twice as quickly as you can.

SELECTING A PREDESIGNED COLOR SCHEME

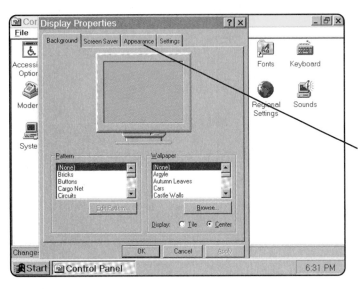

Windows 95 comes with a number of predesigned color schemes. Some of them are set up to give you bigger print, bigger buttons, and bigger icons.

1. **Click** on **Appearance**. The Appearance "tab" will come to the front of the window.

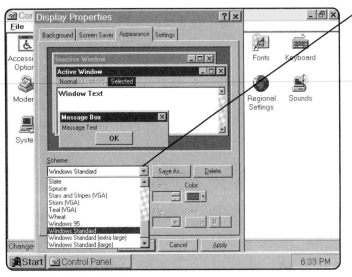

2. **Click** on the ▼ to the right of the Scheme box. A drop-down list of color schemes will appear. Windows Standard is the color scheme that comes with Windows. Your computer may have this color scheme.

3. Press the **Home key** on your keyboard. The highlight bar will go to the top of the list and highlight Brick. The sample screen will change to the Brick color scheme.

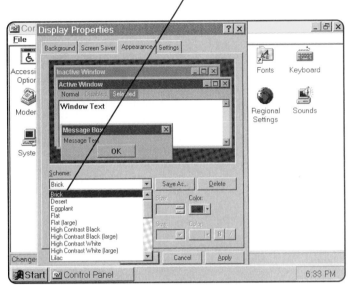

4. Press the ↓ **key** on your keyboard to move the highlight bar down the list one color scheme at a time. As you highlight a new color scheme, the sample screen will change. Give a new color a few seconds to register before you move to the next one, especially if the choice includes a large or extra large option.

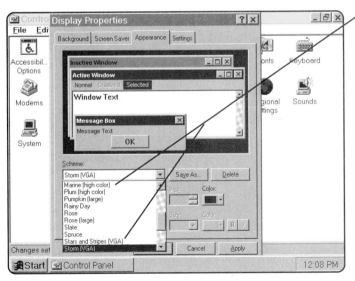

Note: Some choices have "high color" in parentheses after the color scheme. Others have "VGA" after the name. These have to do with the type of monitor (screen) you have and the color card that controls it. Select a scheme you like. If you don't have the appropriate setup for it, the colors will not look clear on your screen. Simply choose another color scheme that looks good.

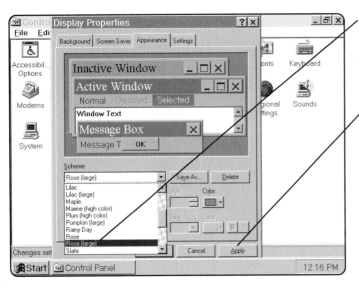

5. When you find a color scheme you like, **click** on the **name** of the scheme. The list will close.

6. Click on **Apply**. The color scheme will be applied to your entire screen.

7. Click on the **Close button** (☒) in the Display Properties window. The window will close, and you'll be back at the Control Panel window.

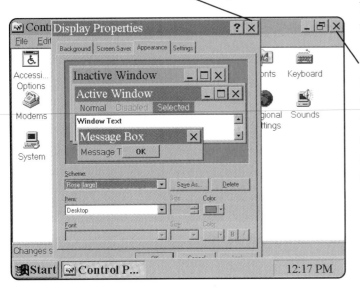

8. Click on the **Close button** (☒) in the Control Panel window. The Control Panel will close, and you'll be back at the opening desktop screen. Your new color scheme will be in effect.

CREATING A CUSTOMIZED COLOR SCHEME

If you don't absolutely love one of the predesigned color schemes, you can design your own. In this section, you'll select one of the predesigned schemes and customize it.

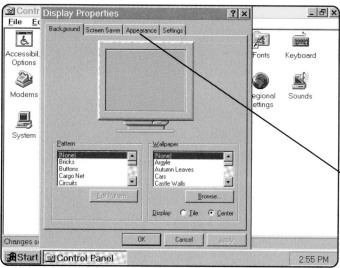
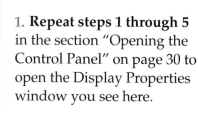

1. **Repeat steps 1 through 5** in the section "Opening the Control Panel" on page 30 to open the Display Properties window you see here.

2. **Click** on **Appearance** to bring the Appearance tab forward.

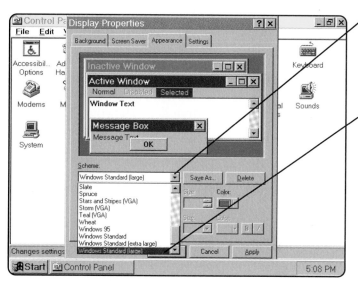

3. **Click** on the ▼ to the right of the Scheme box. A drop-down list of color schemes will appear.

4. **Press** the **End key** on your keyboard. The highlight bar will go to the end of the list. Windows Standard (large) will be highlighted.

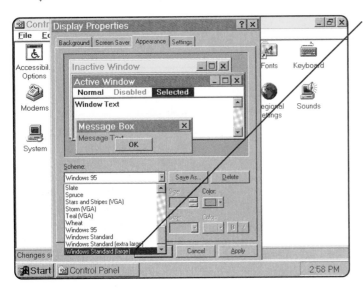

5. Click on **Windows Standard (large).** If you prefer to customize another color scheme, click on that color scheme. The list will close, and the sample window will change to the selected color scheme.

Changing the Color of the Desktop

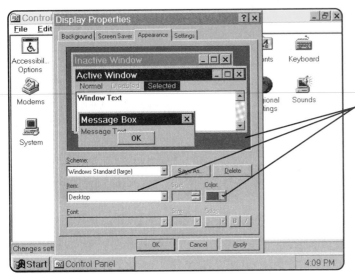

The *desktop* is the opening screen you see when you first boot up Windows. You can make it any color you want.

1. Click on the **desktop area** in the sample window. "Desktop" will appear in the Item box. The color of the desktop will show in the Color box.

2. Click on **other areas** on the sample screen. Notice that the label and color change in the Item and Color boxes. Be sure to click on the desktop again before going on to step 3.

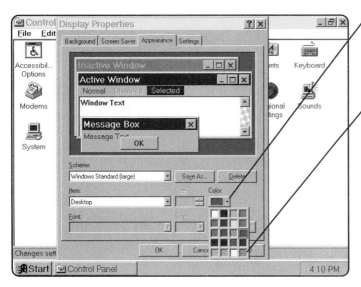

3. **Click** on the ▼ to the right of the Color box. A drop-down color palette will appear.

You should be able to see a button labeled "Other" at the bottom of the color palette. In this example, the bottom of the color palette is hidden by the taskbar. If your palette is partially hidden, go to the next section to hide the taskbar temporarily.

Hiding the Taskbar

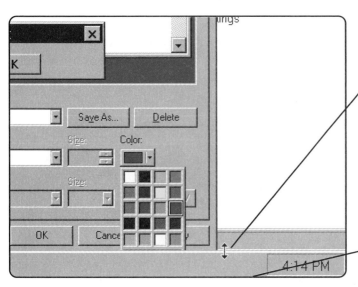

Sometimes the taskbar can interfere with your view. It's easy to hide it temporarily.

1. **Place** your mouse arrow on **top** of the **taskbar border**. The arrow will change shape to the two-headed arrow you see here. You may have to fiddle with the position of the arrow to get it to change shape.

2. **Press and hold** the left mouse button, and then **drag** the arrow down into the bottom of your screen. **Release** the mouse button, and the taskbar will be hidden from view. Don't worry. You'll get it back again at the end of this chapter.

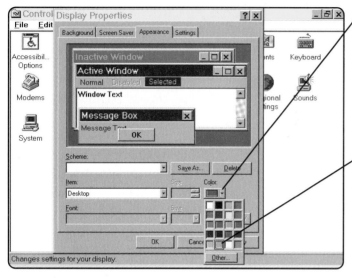

3. Click on the ▼ to the right of the Color box to open the color palette again. (Sometimes the color palette will appear above the Color box instead of below it, as you see here.)

4. Click on the **color** you want your desktop to be. In this example, it is the light blue color that is in the second column, last row. The palette will close, and the desktop will become the color you chose.

Changing the Font

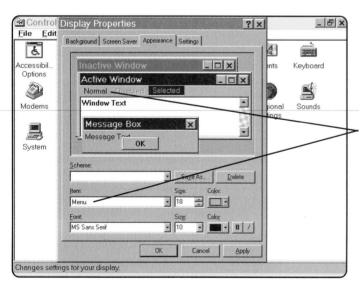

You can change the font, or type, that you see in Windows. In this example, you'll change the font in the menu bar.

1. Click on **Normal** in the sample window. "Menu" will appear in the Item box.

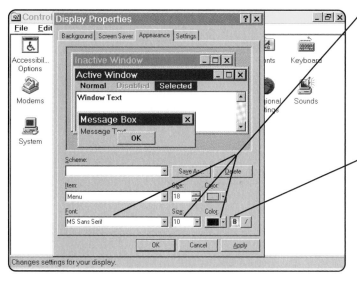

Notice that MS Sans Serif appears in the Font box. The size of the font is 10 and the color is black. You can change any or all of these settings. In this example, you'll make the font boldface.

2. Click on the **B** to the right of the color box. The font in the menu bar will be made boldface.

3. Repeat the steps in this section and the previous section to change other parts of the screen.

SAVING A CUSTOMIZED COLOR SCHEME

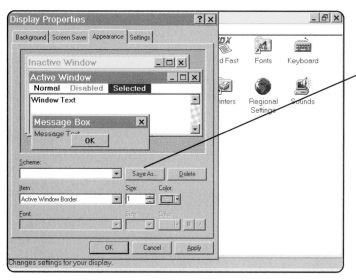

This example shows a customized color scheme.

1. Click on **Save As**. The Save Scheme dialog box will appear.

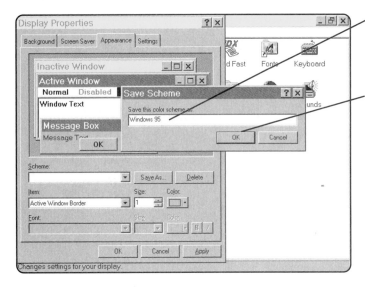

2. Type a **name** for the color scheme. In this example, it is Windows 95.

3. Click on **OK**. The dialog box will close.

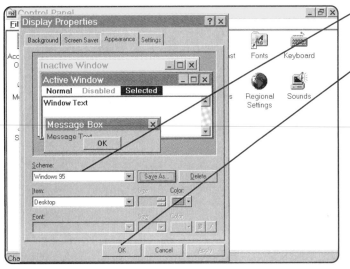

Notice the new name in the Scheme box.

4. Click on **OK**. The dialog box will close, and the color scheme will be applied to your screen.

GETTING THE TASKBAR BACK

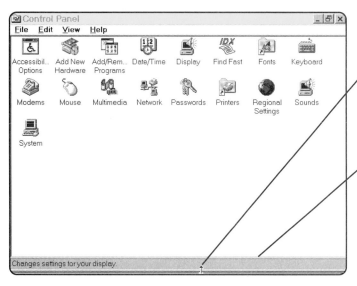

Now you're ready to "unhide" the taskbar.

1. Move the mouse arrow down to the very **bottom** of your screen. You'll see the two-headed arrow again.

2. Press and hold the **left mouse button** and **drag** the arrow **up** the screen to about here. The taskbar will reappear.

CLOSING THE CONTROL PANEL

1. Click on the **Close button** ([×]) to close the Control Panel. You'll be back at the desktop with your new colors.

Customizing the Screen Saver

If you allow an image to remain on your screen for an extended period of time without any changes or movement, it may burn itself into your monitor. Windows provides a *screen saver* to guard against this. A screen saver is a constantly moving graphic image. It appears on your screen when you are interrupted in your work and don't interact with your computer for several minutes. You can customize all aspects of the screen saver. In this chapter, you will do the following:

✔ Customize a screen saver

✔ Create and customize a scrolling marquee

OPENING THE DISPLAY PROPERTIES DIALOG BOX

In Chapter 5, you opened the Display Properties dialog box from the Control Panel. In this section, you'll learn a new way to open it.

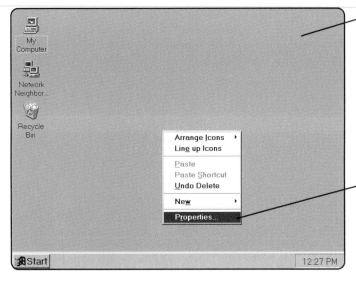

1. **Place** the **mouse arrow** anywhere on the desktop.

2. **Click** the *right* **mouse button**. A pop-up menu will appear. It will probably appear in a different spot from the one in this example.

3. **Click** on **Properties**. The Display Properties dialog box will appear.

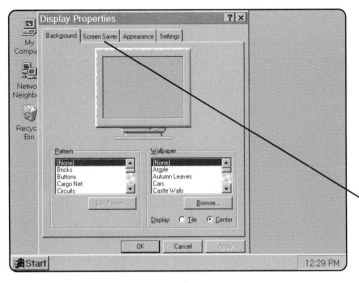

SELECTING A SCREEN SAVER

Windows comes with a variety of screen savers, all of which can be customized. When you get tired of one, you can switch to another.

1. Click on the **Screen Saver tab** to bring it to the front of the dialog box.

2. Click on the ▼ to the right of the Screen Saver box. A drop-down list will appear.

3. Press the ↓ **key** on your keyboard to move through the list one screen saver at a time. Notice that the sample screen shows what the screen saver looks like. Give each screen saver a chance to show up on the sample screen before moving to the next one.

If you upgraded from Windows 3.1, your list may show different choices.

Customizing a Screen Saver

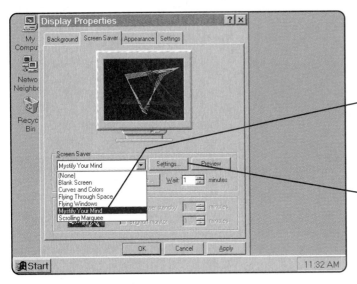

If you select a different screen saver from the one we show, your dialog box will be different.

1. Click on **Mystify Your Mind**. If you upgraded from 3.1, it may be called "Mystify." The list will close.

2. Click on **Settings**. After a pause, the Options to Mystify Your Mind dialog box will appear.

3. Click on the ▼ to the right of the Shape box. A drop-down list will appear.

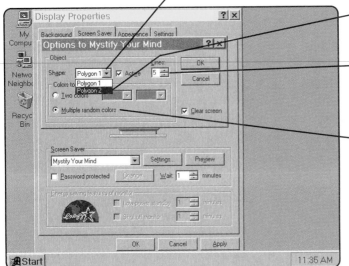

4. Click on **Polygon 2**. The list will close.

5. Click on the ▲ or ▼ to increase or decrease the number of lines in the image.

6. Click on **Multiple random colors** if it doesn't already have a dot in the circle.

Note: You can, of course, customize yours differently.

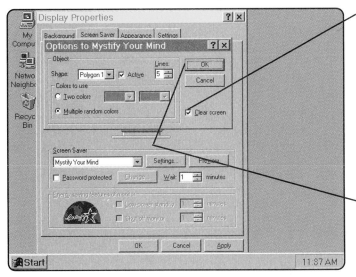

Notice that Clear screen has a ✔ in the box. This will clear your screen so that the screen saver appears against a black background. Your work will not be affected. If you want to superimpose the screen saver over your work, click on the box to *remove* the ✔.

7. When you have made the changes you want, **click** on **OK** to close this dialog box.

If you want to apply this particular screen saver, go to the section entitled, "Applying a Screen Saver," on page 49. If you want to learn how to create a scrolling marquee, continue to the next section.

MAKING A SCROLLING MARQUEE

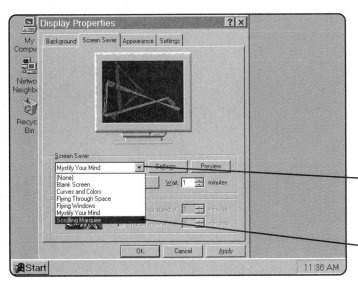

A *marquee* is a message that moves across your screen. Repeat the steps on pages 30 and 31 to open the Display Properties dialog box and bring the Screen Saver tab to the front if it's not already on your screen.

1. **Click** on the ▼ to the right of the Screen Saver box. A drop-down list will appear.

2. **Click** on **Scrolling Marquee**. The list will close.

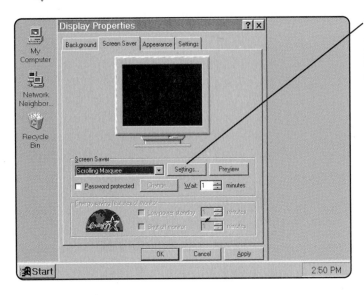

3. **Click** on **Settings**. After a pause, the Options for Scrolling Marquee dialog box will appear.

Customizing the Message

You can type any message you want and then customize the font and the color.

1. **Click** in the **Text box** to place the cursor. On your screen, the text box will be empty.

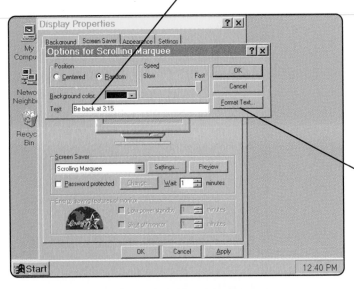

2. **Type** the **message** you want to appear on your screen. In this example, "Be back at 3:15" is the message. You can make the message several sentences long if you want.

3. **Click** on **Format Text**. The Format Text dialog box will appear.

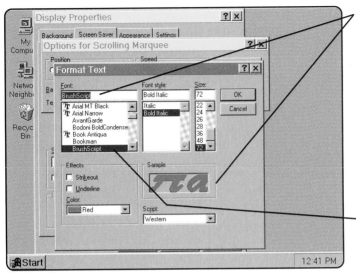

4. **Press** the ↓ **key** on your keyboard to move the highlight bar down the list one font at a time. Notice that a sample of the font appears in the sample box in the lower right corner. The font is very large, so you can't see the entire letter in the sample box.

5. **Click** on the **font** you like best. In this example, it is BrushScript.

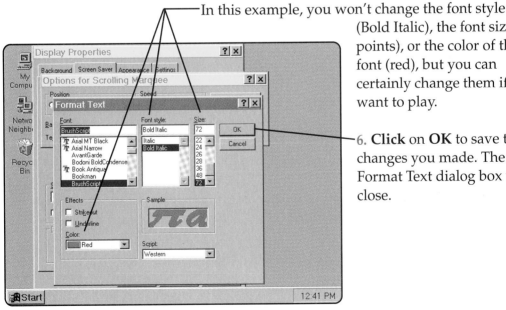

In this example, you won't change the font style (Bold Italic), the font size (72 points), or the color of the font (red), but you can certainly change them if you want to play.

6. **Click** on **OK** to save the changes you made. The Format Text dialog box will close.

7. Click on the ▼ to the right of the Background color box. A drop-down list of colors will appear.

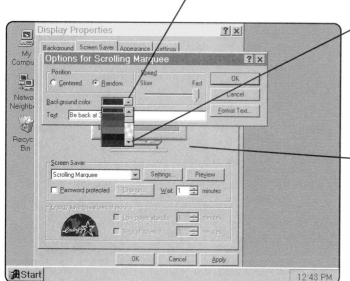

8. Click repeatedly on the ▼ on the scroll bar to move down the list of colors. This is another way, other than pressing the ↓ key, to move (scroll) through a list.

9. In this example, you won't change the background color. **Click anywhere** off the list to close it.

10. Click on **Random** to put a dot in the circle if one is not already there. This will cause the text you typed to appear randomly at the top, middle, and bottom of the screen.

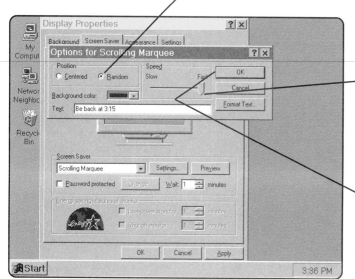

Notice that you can change the speed with which the text scrolls across your screen. In this example, you won't change the speed.

11. Click on **OK** to save the changes you made. The Options for Scrolling Marquee dialog box will close.

APPLYING A SCREEN SAVER

Now that you've customized a screen saver, you're ready to apply it to your screen.

1. Confirm that the screen saver you want is in the Screen Saver box. In this example, it is the Scrolling Marquee. If you want another screen saver, click on the ▼ to open the list.

2. Currently, the screen saver will come on one minute after there has been no activity on your computer. **Click** on the ▲ to increase the amount of time before the screen saver appears.

3. Click on **Apply**.

4. Click on **OK**. The Display Properties dialog box will close, and you'll be back at the desktop.

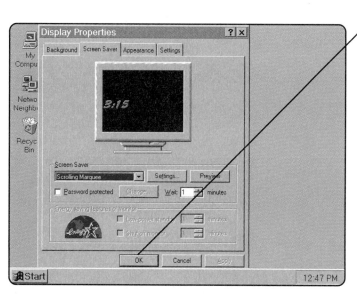

DEACTIVATING A SCREEN SAVER

After you've set up your screen saver and applied it, the screen saver you chose will automatically appear on

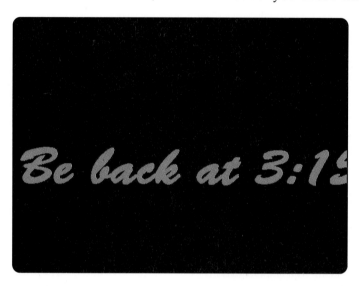

your screen when there has been one minute (or the amount of time you set) when you don't interact with your screen. This will happen no matter what is on your screen.

1. Simply **move** your **mouse** or **click** the **mouse button** to deactivate the screen saver. It will disappear.

REMOVING A SCREEN SAVER

You can remove the screen saver completely.

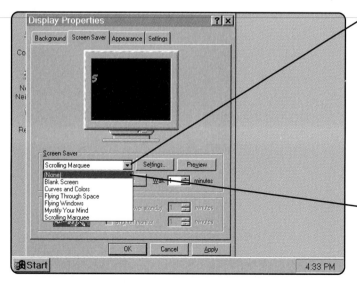

1. Repeat the earlier steps to **open** the **Screen Saver** portion of the Display Properties dialog box you see here.

2. **Click** on the ▼ to the right of the Screen Saver box. A drop-down list will appear.

3. **Click** on [**None**], then **click** on **Apply**, and then **click** on **OK**.

Customizing Your Mouse

You can change the sensitivity of your mouse to clicking speeds. You can also change your mouse to a left-handed mouse. In this chapter, you will do the following:

✔ Switch the functions of the left and right mouse buttons (if appropriate for you)

✔ Customize the mouse's sensitivity to clicking speed

OPENING THE MOUSE PROPERTIES DIALOG BOX

You change the mouse from the Control Panel.

1. **Click** on the **Start button** on the taskbar. A pop-up menu will appear.

2. **Move** the mouse arrow **up** to highlight Settings. A second menu will appear.

3. **Click** on **Control Panel**. The Control Panel window will appear.

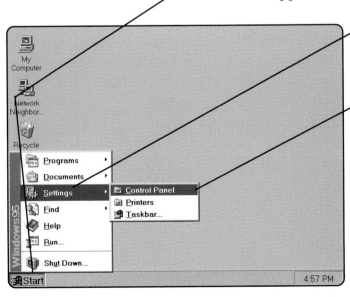

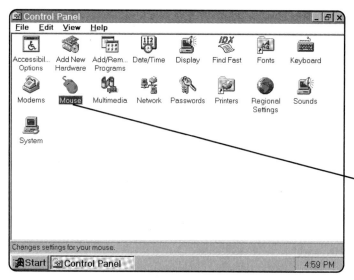

If you opened the Control Panel in Chapter 5 and maximized it, it will fill the screen when you open it for this chapter. If you haven't done Chapter 5 yet, your Control Panel may be smaller in size.

4. Click twice on the **Mouse icon**. Your Mouse icon may be in a different spot on your screen. The Mouse Properties dialog box will appear.

CHANGING TO A LEFT-HANDED MOUSE

If you don't want to change your mouse to a left-handed mouse, skip this section.

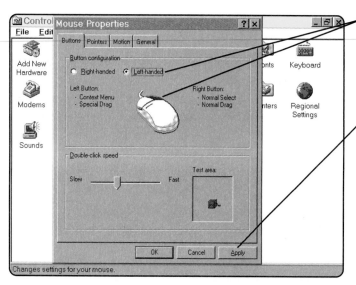

1. Click on **Left-handed** to put a dot in the circle. Notice that the colored mouse button changes from the left to the right side.

2. Click on **Apply**. The change will take effect immediately. When you follow the directions in this book, remember that "click the mouse button" means the right button. When the text refers to the right mouse button, it will mean your left button.

CHANGING THE MOUSE'S SENSITIVITY TO CLICKING SPEED

Single clicks shouldn't give you any problems as long as you place the mouse arrow directly on top of the item you want to click. Clicking twice, or *double-clicking* as it is often called, can be a pain in the neck if your mouse is too sensitive or not sensitive enough. Fortunately, you can change the speed with which you have to click twice.

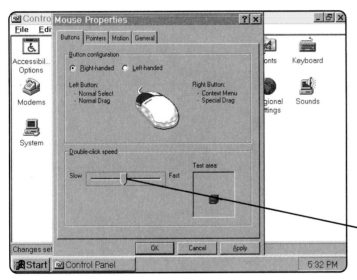

1. Follow the steps at the beginning of this chapter to open the **Mouse Properties dialog box** if it's not already on your screen.

2. Place the mouse arrow on **top** of the **arrow** on the Double-click speed slider bar.

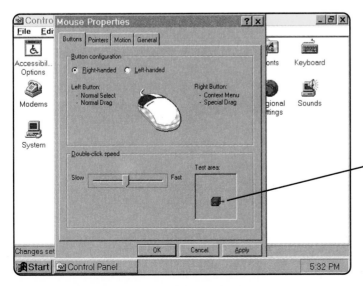

3. Press and hold the mouse button and **drag** the **arrow** toward the appropriate end of the bar. Release the mouse button when the arrow is positioned where you think best.

4. Click twice on the Test area. If you are clicking at the right speed, a little jack-in-the-box will appear.

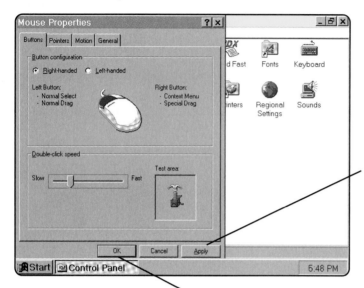

Isn't he cute? If you click twice on Jack, you can put him back into his box.

5. Repeat steps 2 through 4 to test different speeds until you find a comfortable speed.

6. **Click** on **Apply**.

7. **Click** on **OK**. The Mouse Properties dialog box will close. You'll be back at the Control Panel window.

8. **Click** on the **Close button** ([X]) on the Control Panel title bar. The Control Panel will close, and you'll be back at the desktop.

Setting the Date and Time

Windows 95 shows the time on the right side of the taskbar. You can see the day and date simply by resting the mouse arrow on the time button. Although from a personal point of view it's helpful to have the time and date on your screen, these details are also used by Windows programs to record the date and time on files. In this chapter, you will do the following:

✔ Set the date and time

✔ Change the time zone

SEEING TODAY'S DATE

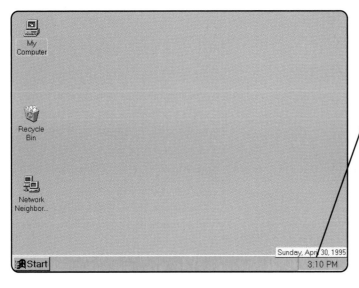

Windows 95 shows the time on the right side of the taskbar. You can see today's date by using the time button.

1. **Place** the mouse arrow on **top** of the **time button**. The day and date will appear as you see here. You may have to fiddle with the placement of the mouse arrow to get the day and date to appear.

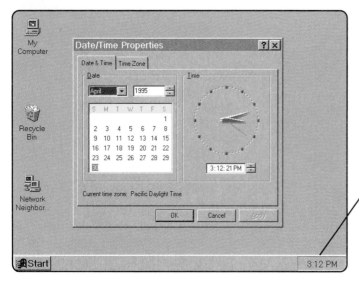

SETTING THE DATE AND TIME

You can set the date and time by using the Date and Time icon in the Control Panel. Here's a shortcut.

1. **Click twice** on the **time button** on the taskbar. The Date/Time Properties dialog box you see here will appear.

Changing the Month, Date, and Year

1. **Click** on the ▼ to the right of the Month box. A drop-down list will appear.

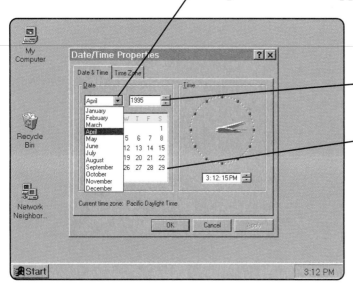

2. **Click** on the **month** you want. The list will close.

3. **Click** on the ▲ or ▼ to change the year.

4. **Click** on the **date** on the calendar you want. The date will be highlighted.

Changing the Time

In Windows there are several ways to accomplish almost everything. When you change the time, you will use two different methods of changing the numbers.

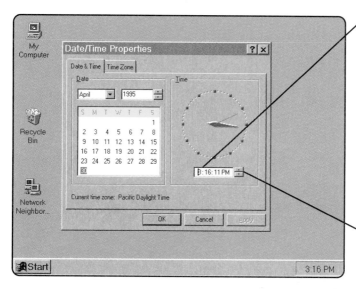

1. **Place** the mouse arrow on **top** of the **hour**. Notice that the arrow changes into the shape of an I-beam in this portion of the window.

2. **Click** the **left mouse button**. This will place a flashing bar (called a *cursor*) in the hour portion of the time.

3. **Click** on the ▲ or ▼ to increase or decrease the hour. Notice that the hands of the clock have stopped moving.

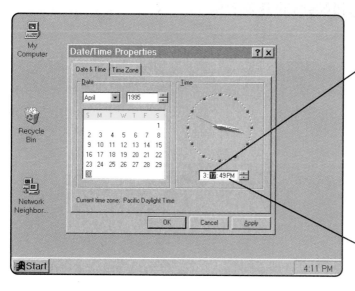

Here's a different way to change a number:

4. **Click twice** on the **minute portion** of the time. The minutes will become highlighted, as you see in this example.

5. **Type** the **new numbers**. They will replace the highlighted numbers.

6. **Repeat steps 4 and 5** to change the seconds.

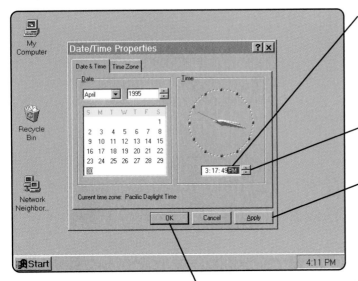

7. Click on AM or PM. It will be highlighted. For some reason, you have to click only once to highlight the AM or PM.

8. Click on the ▲ to change from AM to PM or vice versa.

9. Click on **Apply** to apply the changes. Notice that the hands of the clock will start moving again.

10. If you don't want to change the time zone, **click** on **OK** to close the dialog box. If you do want to change the time zone, skip this step and go to the next section.

CHANGING THE TIME ZONE

If you haven't been following along with this chapter, go back to "Setting the Date and Time" on page 56 to open the Date/Time Properties dialog box you see here.

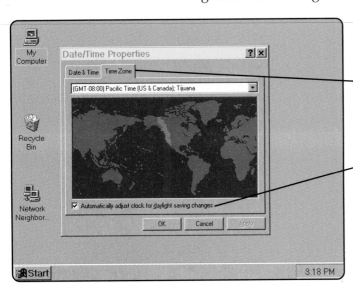

1. Click on the **Time Zone tab** to bring it to the front of the dialog box. The world map you see here will appear.

2. If you do not have daylight savings time in your part of the world, **click on these words** to *remove* the ✔ from the box.

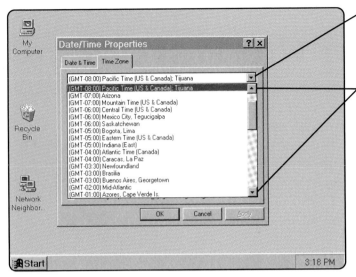

3. **Click** on the ▼ to the right of the time zone box. A drop-down list will appear.

4. **Click repeatedly** on the ▲ or ▼ on the scroll bar to scroll through the list of time zones until you see yours.

5. **Click** on your **time zone**. The list will close.

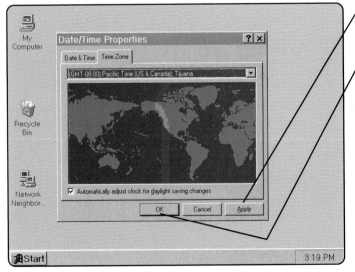

6. **Click** on **Apply** to apply the changes.

7. **Click** on **OK** to close the Date/Time Properties dialog box.

Using the Start Menu

The Start Menu can be a confusing place, especially if you are used to working in Windows 3.1. However, once you have explored its various options, you will find it easy to customize the way you work and to work faster and more easily. In this chapter, you will do the following:

✔ Open programs by using the Run menu

✔ Add a program shortcut to the Programs menu

✔ Remove a program shortcut from the Programs menu

OPENING A PROGRAM WITH RUN

In this section, you will start and close a program by using the Run option. There are three ways to do this.

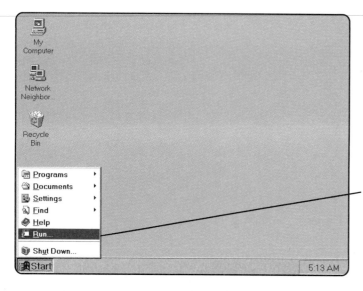

Method #1: Typing the Program Name

1. **Click** on **Start** in the left corner of the taskbar A pop-up menu will appear.

2. **Click** on **Run**. The Run dialog box will appear.

3. **Type** the **name** of the program. See the Following Notes A and B.

Note A: If the program is installed as part of Windows, such as WordPad, Notepad, or Paint, simply type the name of the program. If you're upgrading from 3.1 and you want to get to File Manager, type "winfile" as the name of the program.

Note B: If the program is installed separately, such as WordPerfect or America Online, type the name of the program as well as its *path*, or location, on your hard drive. For example, c:\aol20\waol.exe is the path for America Online. If you don't know the program's path, see Method #2 on the next page.

4. **Click** on **OK**. The program will open. In this example, it is WordPad.

5. **Click** on the **Close button** ([X]) in the right corner of the title bar to close the program.

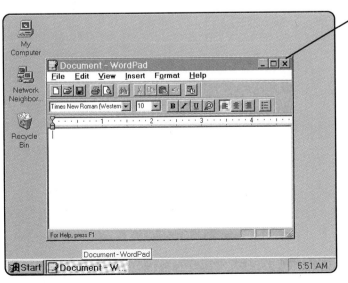

Method #2: Finding the Program's Path

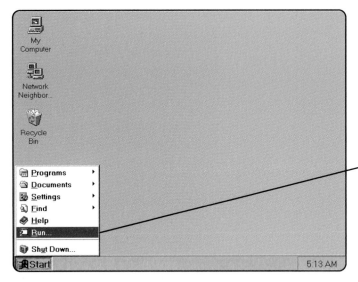

If you don't know the path of the program you want to run, follow the steps below:

1. **Click** on **Start** in the left corner of the taskbar. A pop-up menu will appear.

2. **Click** on **Run**. The Run dialog box will appear.

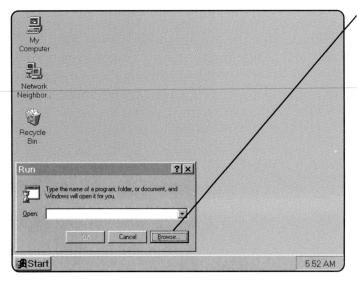

3. **Click** on **Browse**. The Browse dialog box will appear.

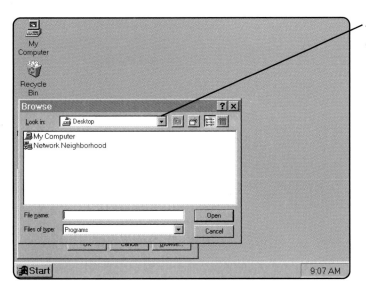

4. Click on the ▼. A drop-down list will appear.

5. Click twice on the **drive** where the file is located. In this example, we clicked on the C:\ drive. A list of folders (directories) will appear in the Browse dialog box.

Note: Since we are on a network, we have a lot of choices. (If you are on a stand-alone machine with only one hard drive, your screen will not look like this one.)

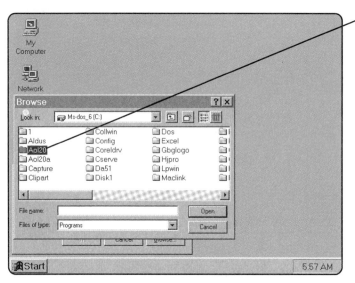

6. Click twice on the **folder** (directory) where the program you want to run is located. A list of files and programs contained in the folder will appear in the Browse dialog box.

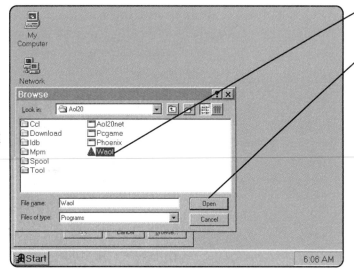

7. Click on the **icon** of the program you want to run.

8. Click on **Open**. The Run dialog box will reappear with the program and its path showing in the Open box, just like the dialog box illustrated in step 2 of the previous section.

9. Click on **OK** in the **Run dialog box** (not shown here). The program will open (in this example, it is America Online).

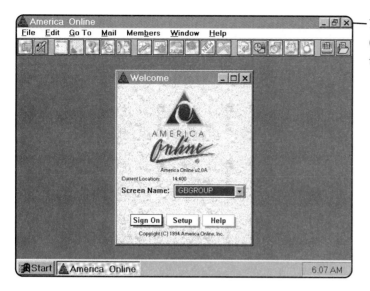

10. Click on the Close button ([X]) in the right corner of the title bar to close the program.

Method #3: Running a Program from the Run List

Every time you run a program by using the Run dialog box, Windows remembers it and puts that program on a list so that you can run it again without the hassle of typing or browsing for the path!

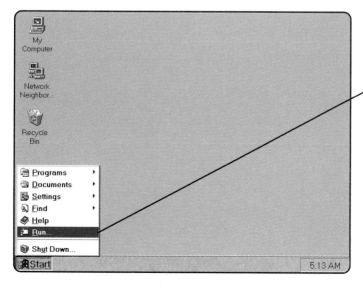

1. **Click** on **Start** in the left corner of the taskbar. A pop-up menu will appear.

2. **Click** on **Run**. The Run dialog box will appear.

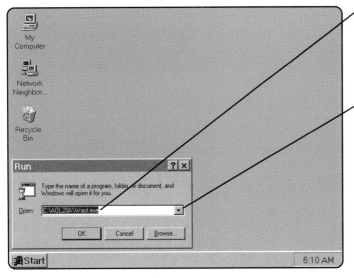

Notice that Windows remembers the last program you ran using this method of starting a program.

3. **Click** on the ▼ to the right of the Open text box. A list will appear.

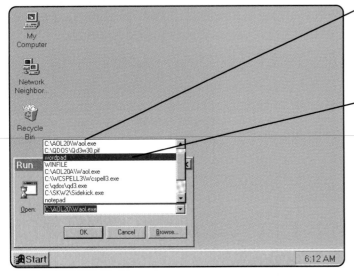

This is a list of all the programs you have opened in the past using the Run option.

4. **Click** on the **name** of the program you want to run. The list will close, and the program will be entered into the Open text box.

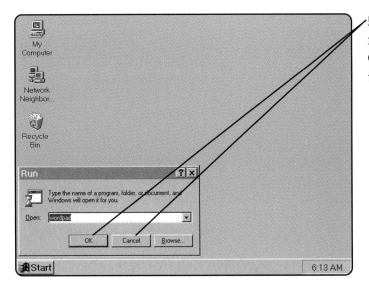

5. **Click** on **OK** if you want to run the program, or **click** on **Cancel** to follow along with the rest of this chapter.

ADDING A PROGRAM SHORT-CUT TO THE PROGRAMS MENU

In this section, you will add a Program shortcut to the Programs menu. A shortcut is simply an icon that launches a program. Windows will create a shortcut icon automatically for any program by following the steps below. In this example, you will create a shortcut for America Online.

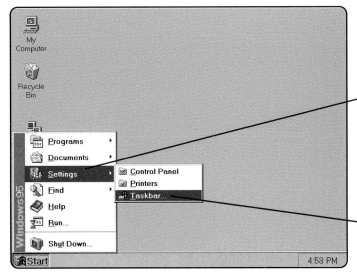

1. **Click** on **Start** in the left corner of the taskbar. A pop-up menu will appear.

2. **Move** the mouse arrow to **Settings**. Another menu will appear. (P.S. for Windows 3.1 folks: You can click on Settings, and the menu will appear.)

3. **Click** on **Taskbar**. The Taskbar Properties dialog box will appear.

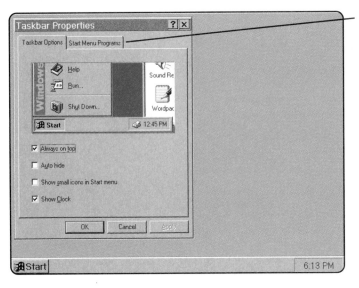

4. Click on **Start Menu Programs**. The Taskbar Properties dialog box will appear.

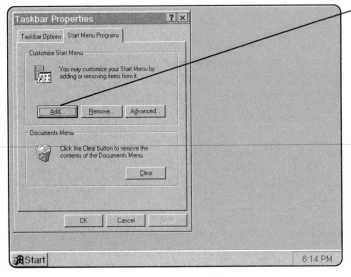

5. Click on **Add**. The Create Shortcut dialog box will appear.

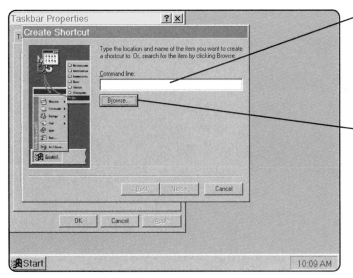

You can type the name and path of the program if you know it and click on OK, or you can follow the steps below.

6. **Click** on **Browse**. The Browse dialog box will appear.

Notice that the Look in text box shows the drive you last visited. If you have been following along in this chapter, your C drive will be shown. If not, this box may show "Desktop." In any case, repeat steps 4 and 5 on page 63 to locate the appropriate drive.

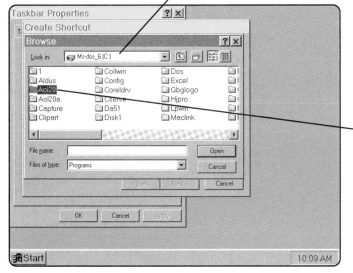

7. **Click twice** on the **folder** (directory) where the program you want to run is located. A list of files and programs contained in the folder will appear in the Browse dialog box.

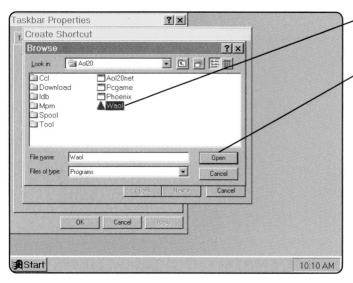

8. **Click** on the **Program** icon to highlight it.

9. **Click** on **Open**. The Create Shortcut dialog box will appear.

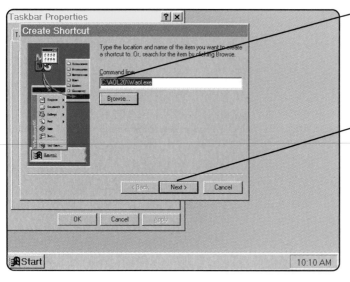

Notice that the path statement or location of the program (c:\AOL20\ Waol.exe) is shown in the Command Line text box.

10. **Click** on **Next**. The Select Program Folder dialog box will appear.

Selecting the Folder for the Program Shortcut

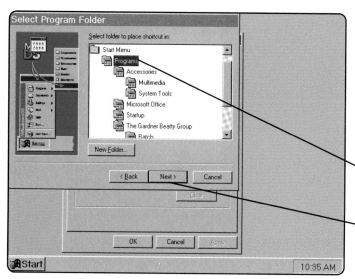

You can put the program shortcut anywhere on the folder tree. In this example, you will put the AOL shortcut in the Programs folder, where it will become one of the Start menu items.

1. Click on the **Programs folder** to highlight it.

2. Click on **Next**. The Select a Title for the Program dialog box will appear.

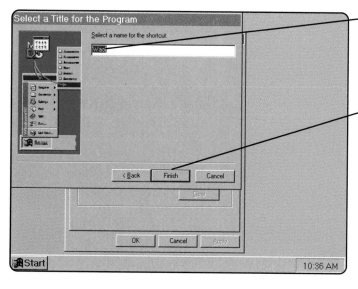

You can rename the program if you want by typing in a new name. In this example, we did not rename it.

3. Click on **Finish**. The Taskbar Properties dialog box will appear.

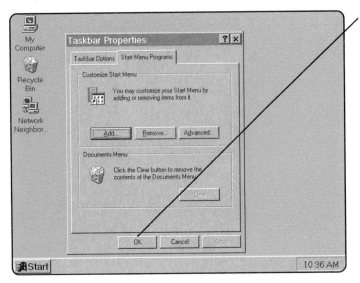

4. **Click** on **OK**. The dialog box will close.

Viewing the New Menu Shortcut

In this section, you will view the new program shortcut you added to the Programs menu.

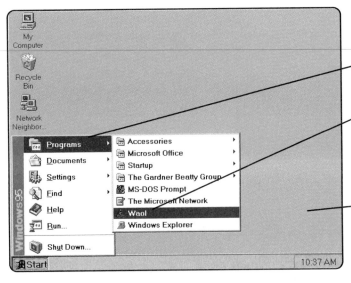

1. **Click** on **Start**. A pop-up menu will appear.

2. **Click** on **Programs**. Another menu will appear.

Voilà! The new "Waol" option (or another program you selected) is now on the Programs menu.

3. **Move** the mouse arrow to **anywhere** on the desktop and **click once**. The menus will close.

REMOVING A PROGRAM SHORTCUT FROM THE PROGRAMS MENU

If you want to remove a program from the Programs menu, it couldn't be easier. In this example, you will remove the AOL program (or another program) from the Programs menu.

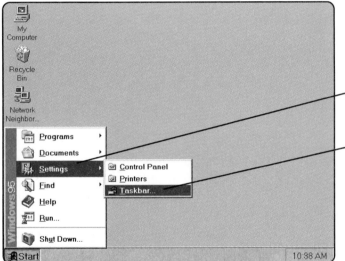

1. Click on **Start**. A pop-up menu will appear.

2. Click on **Settings**. Another menu will appear.

3. Click on **Taskbar**. The Taskbar Properties dialog box will appear.

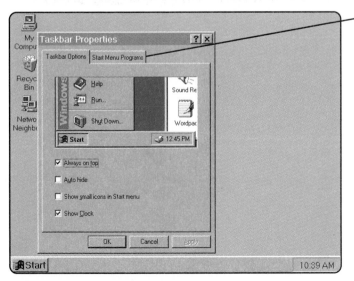

4. Click on **Start Menu Programs**. The Start Menu Programs will come to the foreground.

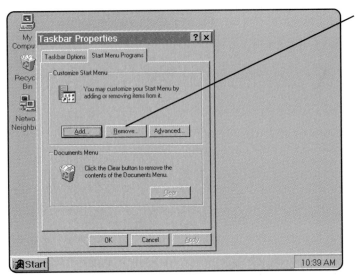

5. **Click** on **Remove**. The Remove Shortcuts/Folders dialog box will appear.

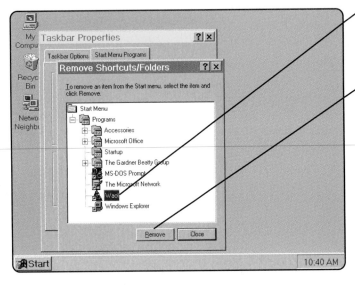

6. **Click** on the **program** you want to remove from the menu to highlight it.

7. **Click** on **Remove**. The program will disappear.

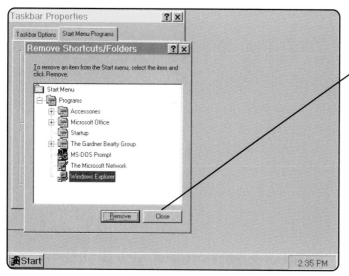

Notice that Waol and its icon are no longer shown.

8. **Click** on **Close**. The Taskbar Properties dialog box will appear.

9. **Click** on the **Close button** (☒). The dialog box will close. The Program will no longer appear on the Programs menu.

RECAPPING

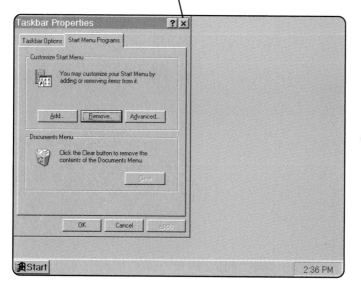

✔ If you are not fond of the Programs menu as a way to start programs, the Run option's list can become your list of favorite programs!

✔ The Programs menu can be a pain if you put too many folders and sub-folders in it. Personally, we launch our most used programs from desktop icons (see Chapter 10) or from the Run option.

Customizing the Desktop

You can customize Windows to work in an almost endless variety of ways. You can even set it up to have the look and feel of the old Windows 3.1 (see Chapter 22 for details). Obviously, we cannot cover all the possibilities in a book like this one, but we can give you the "flavor" of Windows 95's many options. The rest is up to you. In this chapter, you will do the following:

✔ Turn off the Tip of the Day

✔ Put a folder icon on the desktop and remove it

✔ Put a program shortcut icon on the desktop, rename it, and delete it

✔ Put a document shortcut icon on the desktop

✔ Put a program icon in the Startup menu

✔ Move the taskbar to another location and hide it

✔ Set up a desktop icon to open to a specific folder

TURNING OFF THE TIP OF THE DAY

If you would like to get rid of the Tip of the Day that shows up every time you boot up Windows, follow the steps below.

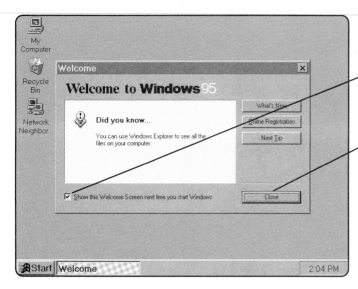

1. **Open Windows** if you have not already done so.

2. **Click** on **Show the Welcome Screen** ... to *remove* the ✔ from the box.

3. **Click** on **Close**. The Welcome window will close. You can always turn it back on by typing "welcome" in the Run menu dialog box (see Chapter 9).

PUTTING A FOLDER ICON ON THE DESKTOP

You can put an icon on the desktop that will launch a folder (directory) with two clicks of the mouse. Very handy if you often open a particular folder containing several frequently used program icons. (Having a folder on the desktop is similar to having a group window in Windows 3.1.)

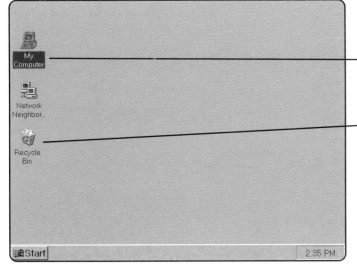

1. **Click twice** on **My Computer**. The My Computer window will open.

Note: Your desktop may have more icons on it than ours. That's because we deleted several icons we didn't want. See the section "Deleting Desktop Icons," later in this chapter.

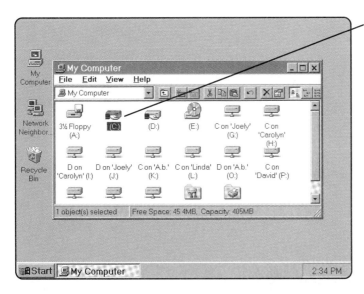

2. **Click twice** on the hard drive icon where your folder is located. In this example, we clicked on our C drive icon (C:). The (C:) window will appear.

Note: If your window fills the screen, click on the Restore button ([image]) in the right corner of the title bar to get it to this size so that you can still see the desktop.

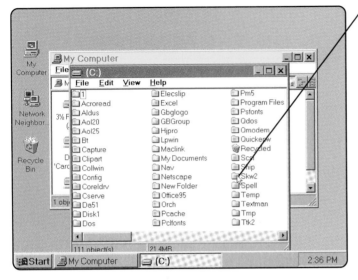

3. Move the mouse arrow to the **folder** (directory) icon you want to move to the desktop. In this example, we chose our Sidekick for Windows (Skw2) folder.

Note: Your view in this window may be different from the one shown here. See Chapter 16, page 171, the section entitled "Changing the View," if you want to duplicate this view.

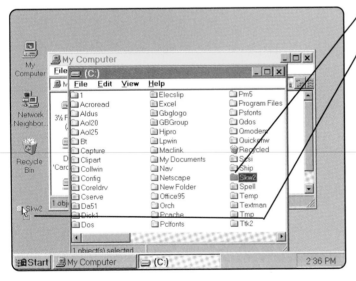

4. Click on the **folder icon**.

5. Press and hold the mouse button (a plus sign (+) may appear attached to the arrow) as you **drag** the **icon** to the desktop.

6. Release the mouse button. The folder icon will now appear on the desktop.

Note: For those who are familiar with the older versions of Windows, this folder icon works like one of the group icons in Windows 3.1.

Closing Folder Windows

In this section, you will close the windows you opened to clear your desktop screen.

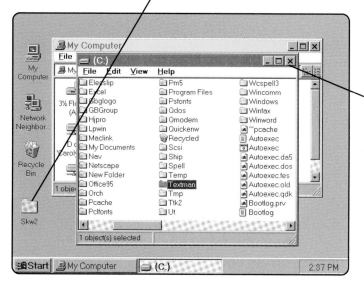

1. **Click** on the **Close button** ([X]) in the right corner of the title bar to close the window for the C: drive.

2. **Click** on the **Close button** ([X]) in the right corner of the title bar to close the My Computer window.

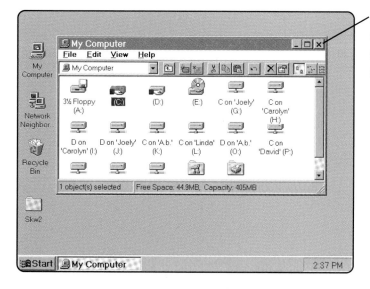

REMOVING A FOLDER ICON FROM THE DESKTOP

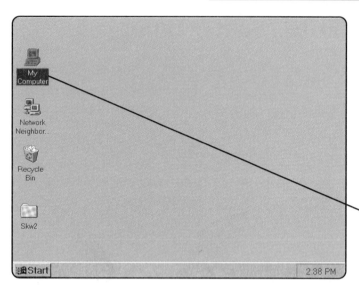

Removing a folder icon from the desktop couldn't be easier.

Warning: Do not right-click your mouse and use the Delete command. You will erase the folder from your hard drive!

1. **Click twice** on **My Computer**. The My Computer window will open.

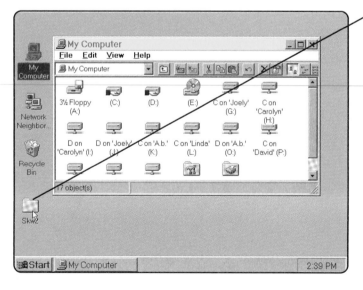

2. **Move** the mouse arrow to the **folder icon** on your desktop.

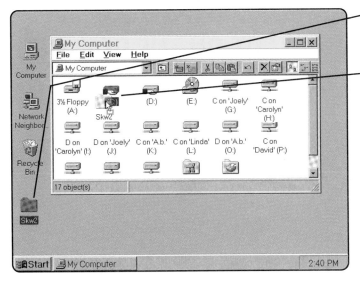

3. **Click** on the **folder icon** (in this example, Skw2).

4. **Press** and **hold** the mouse button as you **drag** the **icon** to the C drive icon (C:) in the My Computer window.

5. **Release** the mouse button. The Skw2 folder icon will disappear and return to its original location on your hard drive.

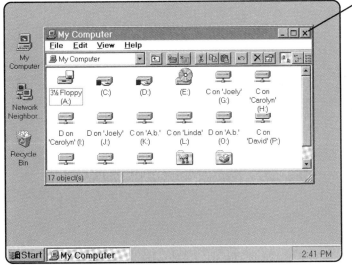

6. **Click** on the **Close button** ([×]) in the right corner of the title bar to close the window.

PUTTING A PROGRAM SHORTCUT ON THE DESKTOP

You can set up your desktop with shortcut icons to launch your most used programs. This will save you from having to wade through layers of menus to start a program. Two clicks and you are there!

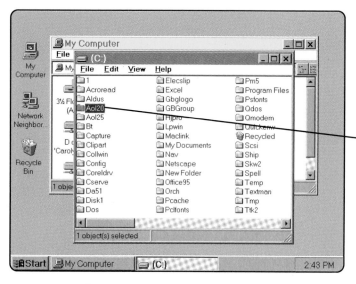

1. **Repeat steps 1 and 2** on page 77 in the section entitled "Putting a Folder Icon on the Desktop" to open your C drive window (C:), as shown here.

2. **Click twice** on the **folder** containing the program you want to "shortcut" (launch from the desktop with a shortcut icon). A window containing the contents of the folder will open. In this example, we clicked on the Aol20 folder icon.

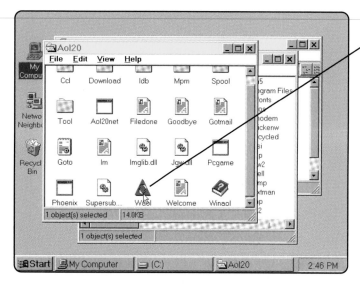

3. **Move** the mouse arrow to the **program icon**. In this example, it is the Waol program icon.

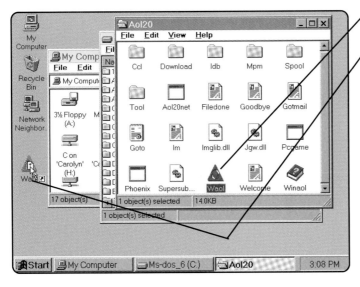

4. **Click** on the **program icon**.

5. **Press** and **hold** the mouse button (a plus sign (+) will appear attached to the arrow) as you **drag** the **icon** to the desktop.

6. **Release** the mouse button. The program shortcut icon will now appear on the desktop.

Note: If the above steps, for some unknown reason, did not create a shortcut icon for the program, move the program icon back to the folder. You can create a shortcut icon another way by clicking the right mouse button on the program icon and then clicking on Create Shortcut. You would then follow steps 1 through 6 above to put the newly created shortcut icon on the desktop.

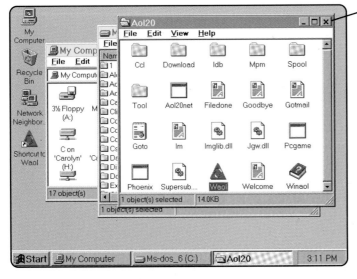

7. **Click** on the **Close buttons** (⊠s) of the following windows to close them:

⊠ Aol20

⊠ (C:)

⊠ My Computer

RENAMING A DESKTOP ICON

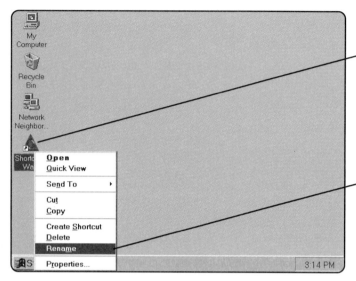

Renaming is easy to do.

1. Move the mouse arrow to the icon you want to rename.

2. Click the **right mouse button**. A pop-up menu will appear.

3. Click on **Rename**. The name under the icon will change to a white background.

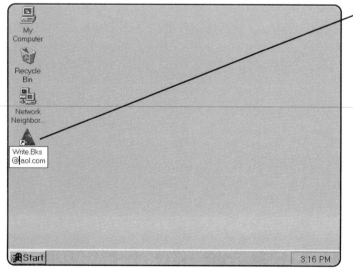

4. Type the **new name** and then **click anywhere** on the desktop. The new name will appear at the bottom of the icon.

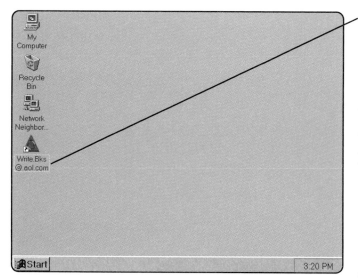

Notice the new name for the America Online icon.

You can send mail to us at this Internet address: write.bks@aol.com. We always welcome comments and suggestions about our books.

DELETING DESKTOP ICONS

Deleting a shortcut icon does not delete the program. You can tell a shortcut by the little arrow that appears in its lower left corner. It's a good idea to be more cautious about deleting icons that are not shortcut icons because this will remove the program from your hard drive if you clear the Recycle Bin. You would then have to reinstall it to get it back. You cannot delete the My Computer and Recycle Bin icons. If you have a network, you cannot delete the network icon.

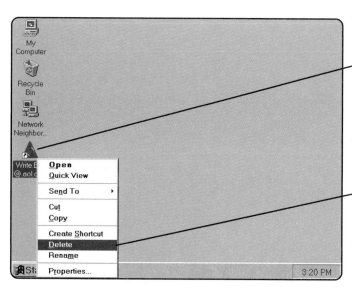

1. Click on the **icon** to highlight it.

2. Click on the **right mouse button**. A pop-up menu will appear.

3. Click on **Delete**. The Confirm File Delete dialog box will appear.

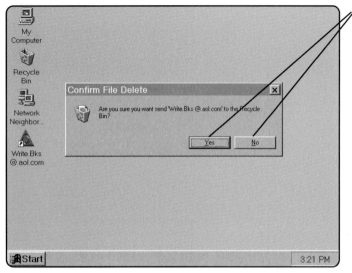

4. Click on **Yes** if you want to delete it, or **click** on **No** if you change your mind. In this example, we did not delete the American Online icon since it is a program we use frequently.

PUTTING A DOCUMENT ICON ON THE DESKTOP

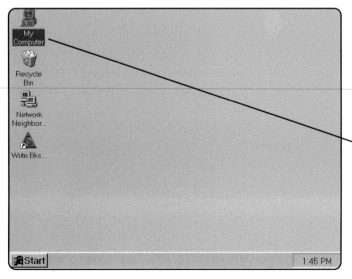

In addition to folder and program icons, you can also put on your desktop an icon that opens a specific document when you click on it.

1. Click twice on **My Computer**. The My Computer window will appear.

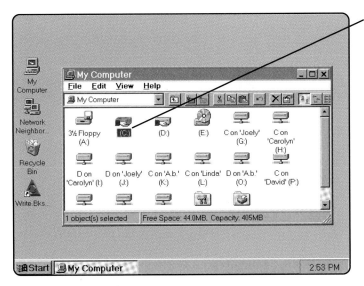

2. **Click twice** on the **C drive icon** (in this example, (C:)). The (C:) window will appear.

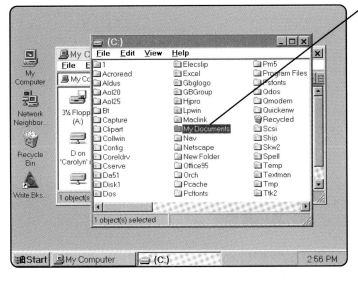

3. **Click twice** on the **folder icon**. In this example, we clicked on a folder entitled My Documents. Thus, the My Documents dialog box will appear.

If you do not have a folder called My Documents, you can create one (see Chapter 16, page 172, the section entitled, "Making a New Folder"), or you can use another folder to follow along.

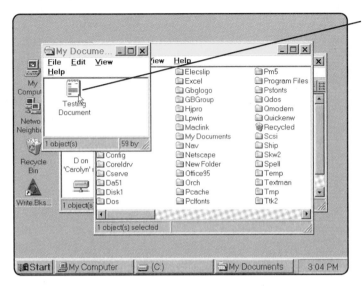

4. Move the mouse arrow to the **document icon** you want to make into a shortcut. (For this example, we created a document in WordPad to illustrate the process.)

5. Click on the **document icon** to highlight it.

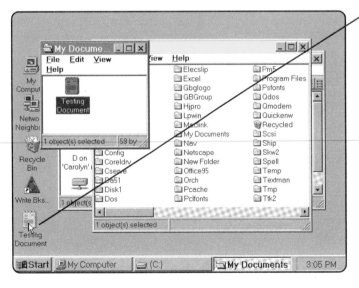

6. Press and **hold** the mouse button (a plus sign (+) will appear attached to the arrow) as you **drag** the **icon** to the desktop.

7. Release the mouse button. The document icon will now appear on the desktop.

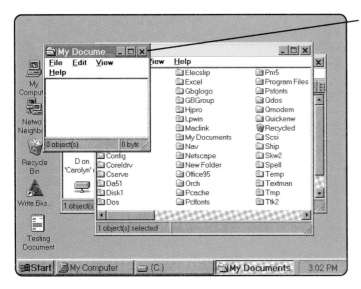

8. **Click** on the **Close buttons** ([x]s) of the following windows to close them:

[x] My Document

[x] (C:)

[x] My Computer

DELETING A DOCUMENT SHORTCUT ICON

When you are not working with a document on a daily basis, a shortcut icon for the document takes up space on your desktop. In this section, you'll delete a shortcut icon.

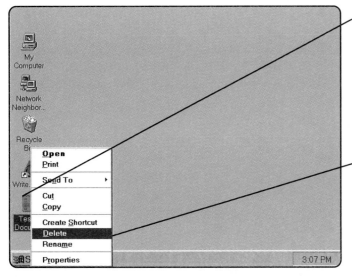

1. **Click** on the **document icon** you want to delete to highlight it.

2. **Click** the **right mouse button**. A pop-up menu will appear.

3. **Click** on **Delete**. The Confirm File Delete dialog box will appear.

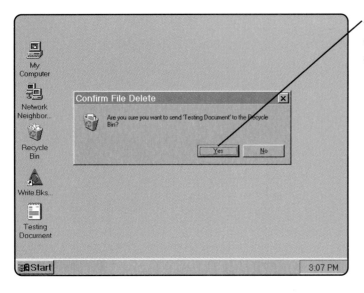

4. **Click** on **Yes**. The document shortcut icon will disappear.

PUTTING A PROGRAM ICON IN THE STARTUP MENU

You can put a program icon into the Startup menu so that each time you boot up Windows, the program will be launched automatically. In this example, you will put WordPad in the Startup menu.

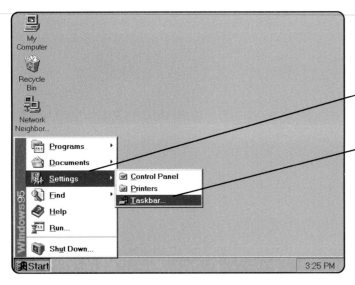

1. **Click** on **Start** in the left corner of the taskbar. A pop-up menu will appear.

2. **Click** on **Settings**. Another menu will appear.

3. **Click** on **Taskbar**. The Taskbar Properties dialog box will appear.

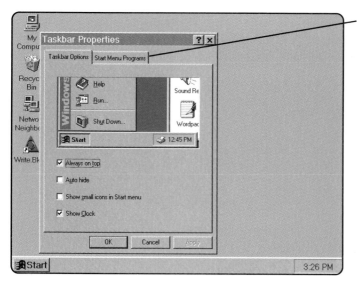

4. **Click** on **Start Menu Programs**. The Customize Start Menu dialog box will come to the front.

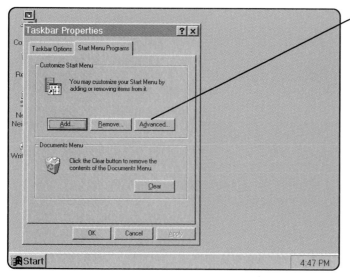

5. **Click** on **Advanced**. The Exploring - Start Menu window will appear.

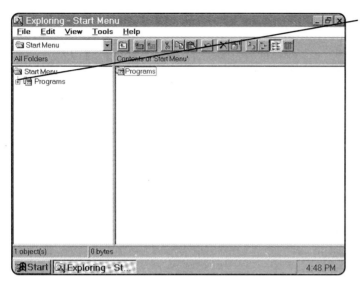

6. Click on the **expand box** (⊞) to the **left** of the **Programs icon**. The folder tree will expand, showing the subfolders in the Programs menu.

7. Click on **Accessories**. The programs contained in the Accessories folder will be shown in the Contents of 'Accessories' box.

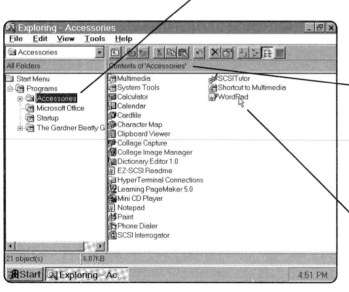

Note: Depending on how your computer has been organized, the contents of your Accessories folder may be different from what is shown here.

8. Move the mouse arrow to **WordPad**.

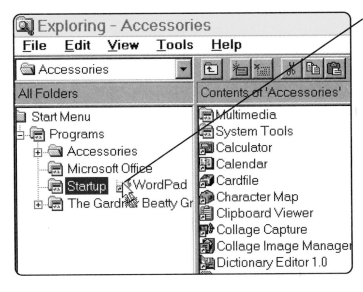

9. **Press** and **hold** the mouse button (a plus sign (+) will appear attached to the arrow) as you **drag** the **icon** to the Startup icon in the All Folders box.

10. **Release** the mouse button. The WordPad icon will now disappear into the Startup folder.

Viewing the Results

Any program listed in the Startup menu will automatically start up when you start Windows. If we did everything correctly, WordPad should be in the Startup menu. Let's see.

Notice that WordPad is no longer in the Contents of 'Accessories' box.

1. **Click** on the **Close button** ([X]) in the right corner of the title bar to close the dialog box.

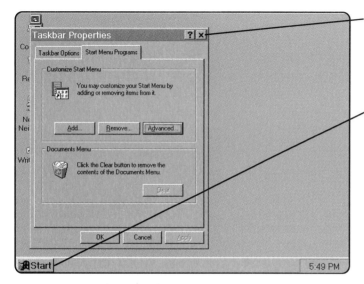

2. Click on the **Close button** ([×]) in the right corner of the title bar to close the dialog box.

3. Click on **Start**. A pop-up menu will appear.

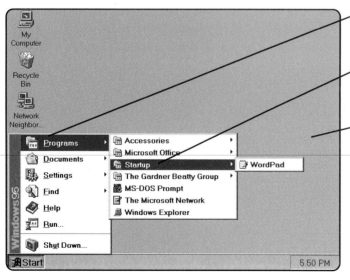

4. Click on **Programs**. Another menu will appear.

5. Click on **Startup**. Voilà! WordPad is there!

6. Click anywhere on the desktop to close the menus.

Removing a Program from the Startup Menu

You can remove any program from the Startup menu by following the previous steps in this section. Simply drag the program's icon from the Startup folder to another folder.

MOVING THE TASKBAR

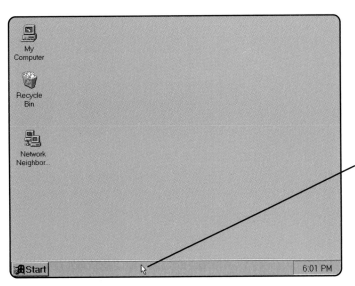

If you do not like the task bar at the bottom of your screen, you can move it very easily to either side of the screen or to the top. In this example, you will move the taskbar to the top of your screen.

1. **Move** the mouse arrow to **any clear space** on the **taskbar**, as shown here. Be sure not to move to a program button.

2. **Press** and **hold** the mouse button as you **drag** it to the **top** of your screen. A white line will appear, first on the side and then horizontally, as shown here.

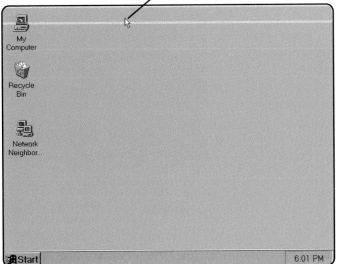

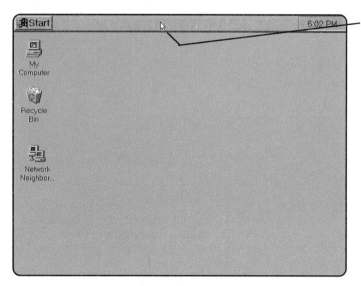

3. **Release** the mouse button. The taskbar will move to the top of the screen, as shown here.

4. **Repeat steps 1 through 3** in reverse to move the taskbar back to the bottom.

REMOVING THE TASKBAR FROM VIEW

If you do not want the taskbar showing on your screen all the time, you can hide it from view and get it back any time you need it with a simple mouse movement.

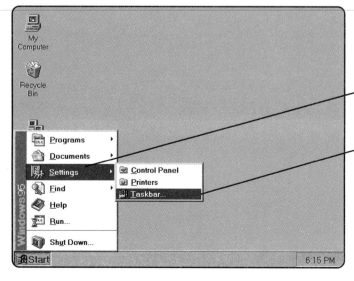

1. **Click** on **Start** in the left corner of the taskbar. A pop-up menu will appear.

2. **Click** on **Settings**. Another menu will appear.

3. **Click** on **Taskbar**. The Taskbar Properties dialog box will appear.

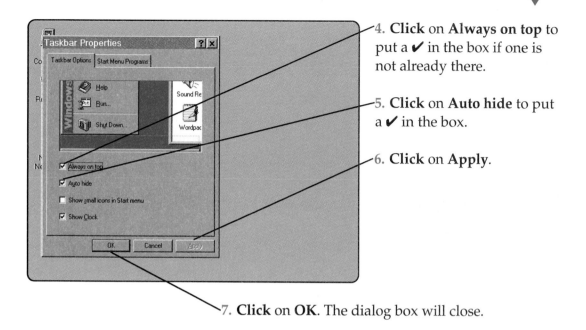

4. **Click** on **Always on top** to put a ✔ in the box if one is not already there.

5. **Click** on **Auto hide** to put a ✔ in the box.

6. **Click** on **Apply**.

7. **Click** on **OK**. The dialog box will close.

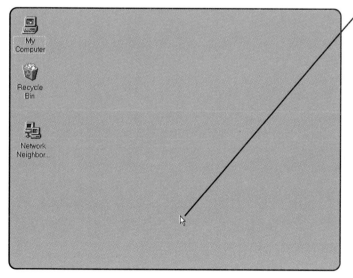

8. **Move** the mouse arrow anywhere on the desktop. The taskbar is gone. How do you get it back when you need it? Go on to the next page.

GETTING THE HIDDEN TASKBAR BACK

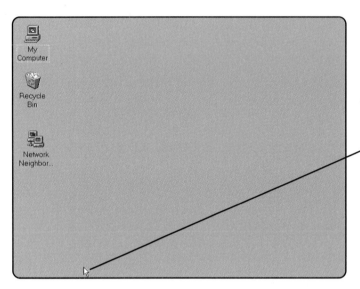

You can get the taskbar back any time you want by a simple mouse movement. You can do this at any time from any program you have running.

1. **Move** the mouse arrow **toward** the **bottom** of the desktop.

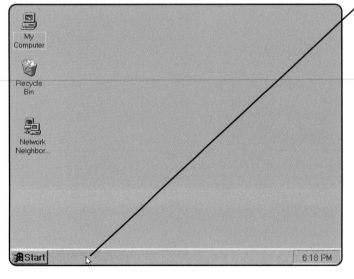

2. **Continue** to **move** the mouse arrow until the taskbar reappears.

Note A: To hide the taskbar, simply move the mouse arrow onto the desktop.

Note B: If you want to get the taskbar back permanently, repeat steps 1 through 6 in the previous section of this chapter to *remove* the ✔ from the Auto hide box.

Notice that we have added several shortcut icons to our desktop.

OPENING A PROGRAM TO A SPECIFIC FOLDER

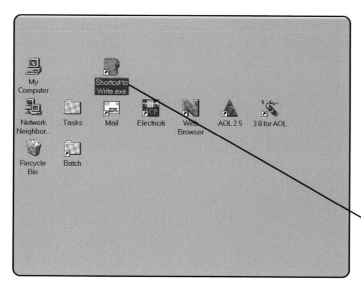

If you want a program to open to a specific folder, you can set up its shortcut icon to do just that (in Windows 3.1, this was called opening to a working directory). In this section, you will set up a shortcut icon to open WordPad in the My Documents directory.

1. **Repeat steps 1 through 6** in the section in this chapter entitled "Putting a Program Shortcut on the Desktop" to create a shortcut icon for WordPad. Note that the program icon for WordPad is contained in the Windows folder and is called Shortcut to Write.

2. **Move** the mouse arrow to the **Shortcut to Write icon** and press the **right mouse button**. A menu will appear.

3. **Click** on **Properties**. The Shortcut to Write Properties dialog box will appear.

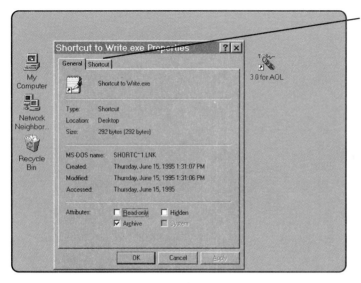

4. Click on **Shortcut** to bring the tab to the front.

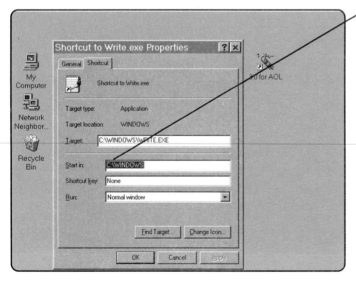

5. Click twice in the **Start in** text box to highlight it.

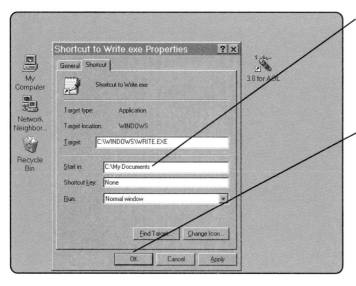

6. Type the path (location and name) of the folder you want to set up WordPad to open to. In this example, we typed C:\My Documents.

7. Click on **OK**. The dialog box will close.

VIEWING A CUSTOMIZED DESKTOP

Here are three ideas for a customized desktop (in Chapter 22, you can pick up more tips on customizing):

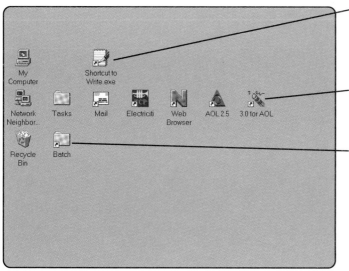

❶ A desktop icon set up to open to a specific directory. (You will learn to open WordPad in Chapter 12.)

❷ Icons for some of our favorite programs ready to launch on the desktop.

❸ A folder icon on the desk-top containing our DOS Batch Files (for those of us who still use them).

WINDOWS 95

Part III: Using Windows Programs

Exploring Help

Windows 95 includes an on-line help program. *On-line* means that you get the information through your computer as opposed to looking it up in a book. The Help program contains some neat hypertext links. If you've heard of hypertext but don't have a clue what it means, this is a great place to see it in action. In this introduction to Help, you will do the following:

✔ Explore Help

OPENING HELP FROM THE DESKTOP

You can open the Help program directly from the desktop.

1. **Click** on the **Start button** in the taskbar. A pop-up menu will appear.

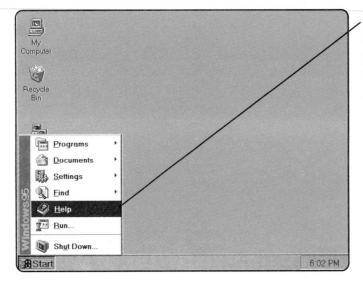

2. **Click** on **Help**. You'll see an hourglass, and, after a brief pause, the Help Topics: Windows Help window will appear.

3. Click on **Contents** to bring it to the front of the window if it's not already.

You'll see a list of topics.

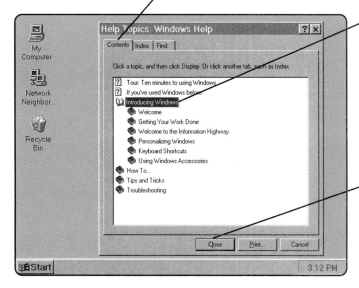

4. Click twice on **Introducing Windows**. The little book to the left will open, and the list will expand to show several subtopics. In this example, you won't explore these particular topics. In the next step, you'll close this topic.

5. Click on **Close** while the topic is highlighted. The book and the list will close. You can also click twice on the open book to close the topic.

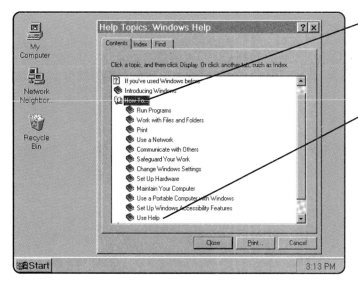

6. Click twice on **How To**. The book will open, and the list will expand to show all the How To topics.

7. Click twice on **Use Help**. A list of subtopics will appear.

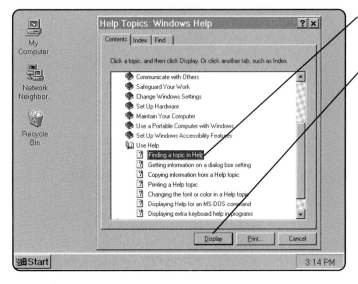

8. Click *once* on **Finding a topic in Help** to highlight it.

9. Click on **Display**. (This is the same thing as clicking twice on the highlighted item.) The Windows Help dialog box you see in the following example will appear.

Returning to the Help Topics Window

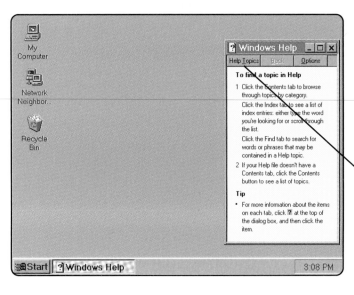

If this window gives you the information you need, you can close it by clicking on the Close button (⊠) on the right side of the title bar. If you want to search for more help, see the next step.

1. Click on **Help Topics**. You'll be returned to the Help Topics window.

USING THE INDEX

Help has an index of topics, like the index in a book. However, it's easier to use than a book because you simply type a topic and Windows will do the hunting.

1. **Repeat steps 1 and 2** at the beginning of this chapter to open the Help Topics window you see here (if it's not already on your screen.)

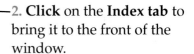

2. **Click** on the **Index tab** to bring it to the front of the window.

3. **Type margins**. The highlight bar will go to the first instance of margins in the index.

4. **Click** on **Display**. The topic will be displayed.

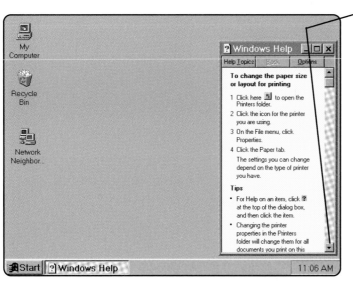

5. **Click repeatedly** on the ▼ on the scroll bar to scroll through the text. You'll find, however, that "margins" isn't even mentioned. You sometimes have to be patient and/or creative in searching Help. This particular topic does have a point of interest, however. See the next section for an example of a hypertext link.

6. **Click** on the ▲ to return to the top of the dialog box.

USING A HYPERTEXT LINK

A *hypertext* link is an automatic connection to another piece of information or another window.

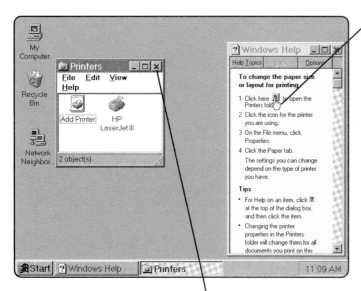

1. Place the mouse arrow on **top** of the **button** after "Click here." The mouse arrow will change to a cute little hand.

2. Click on the **button**. You'll see an hourglass, and after a brief pause the Printers window you see to the left will appear. In this example, you won't use the Printers window, so in the next step you'll close it.

3. Click on the **Close button** ([X]) on the right side of the Printers title bar.

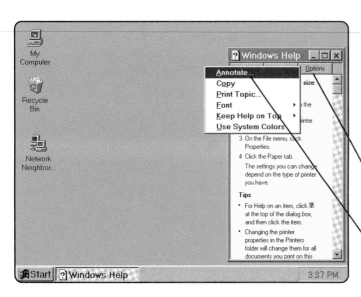

MAKING A NOTE TO YOURSELF

You can write yourself a note about a Help topic.

1. Click on **Options**. The pop-up menu you see here will appear.

2. Click on **Annotate**. The Annotate dialog box will appear.

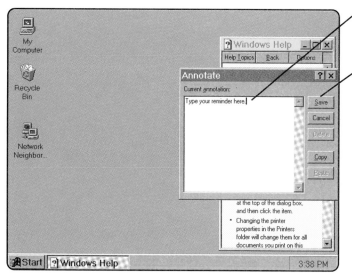

3. **Type your reminder** in the window.

4. **Click** on **Save**. The Annotate dialog box will close, and a little paper clip will appear to the left of the topic in the Help window.

Using a Note

Once you've created a note, it's easy to access it.

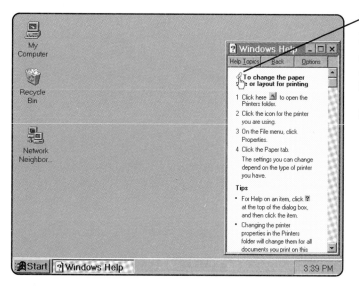

1. **Click** on the **paper clip**. Notice that the mouse arrow changes to the hand when you point at the paper clip. The Annotate window will appear again.

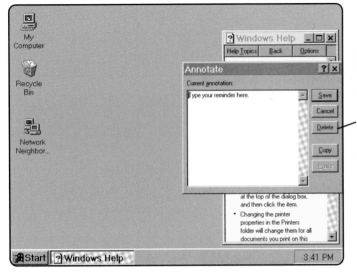

In this example, you'll delete the note. You'll learn about copying and pasting in Chapter 12, "Writing a Memo in WordPad."

2. **Click** on **Delete**. The note will be deleted from the topic.

GOING BACK TO A PREVIOUS TOPIC

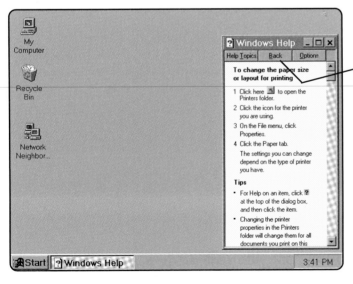

It's easy to go back to a previous topic.

1. **Click** on **Back** to go back to the previous level of Help topics.

If your **Back** button is grayed out, go on to step 2.

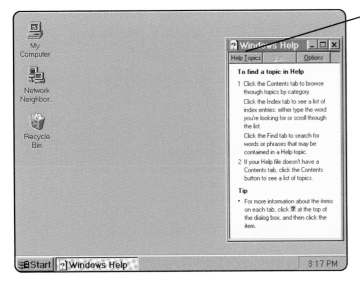

2. **Click** on **Help Topics** to go back to the main Help Topics window.

USING FIND FOR THE FIRST TIME

The first time you use the Find feature, Windows 95 will build the list of words, or database, that the Find feature searches.

1. **Open** the **Help Topics Window** if it is not already on your screen.

2. **Click** on the **Find tab** to bring it to the front of the Help Topics dialog box. You'll see a moving icon of a pen writing in a book, then the message box you see here will appear. If someone has already used the Find feature, you won't see this message box or the two on the next page. Go to page 113.

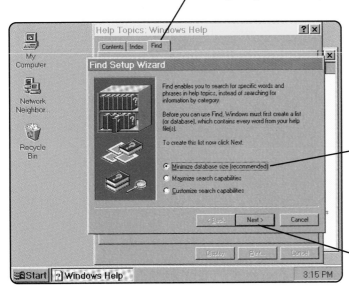

3. **Click** on **Minimize database size** (recommended) to put a dot in the circle if one is not already there.

4. **Click** on **Next**.

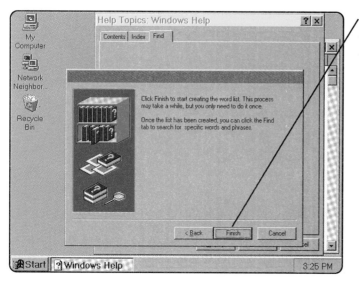

5. **Click** on **Finish**. The window you see below will appear.

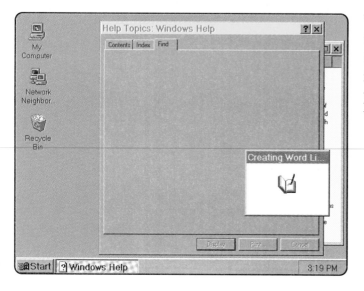

When the pen stops writing, the database is finished. (Don't you love these moving images?) The Find window you see in the next example will appear.

IDENTIFYING ITEMS

If you don't understand the purpose of an item, Windows 95 has a nifty identification function. This section assumes that you have clicked on the Find tab in the Help Topics window.

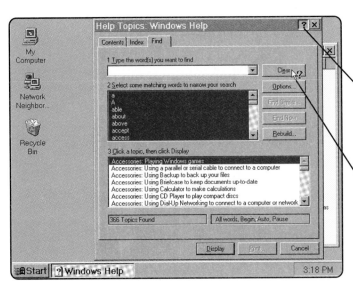

1. **Click** on the ? in the title bar. A question mark will appear next to the mouse arrow.

2. **Click** on the **item** you want defined. In this example, it is the Clear button. A definition of the item will appear.

Pretty neat, don't you think?

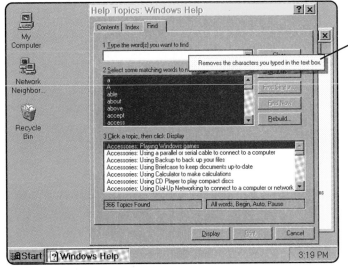

3. **Click** the **mouse button** to close the definition.

USING THE FIND FUNCTION

The Find function in Help will find all occurrences of a specific word in the Help material that comes with Windows 95. This section assumes that you have the Help Topics window open, as you see here.

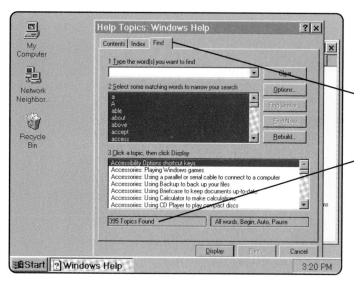

1. Click on the **Find tab** to bring it to the front if you have not already done so.

Notice that the text at the bottom of the window tells you the number of topics in the Help library. Your number may be different.

In this example, you'll use Find to look for all occurrences of the word "printer."

2. Click in the **Find text box** and **type printer**.

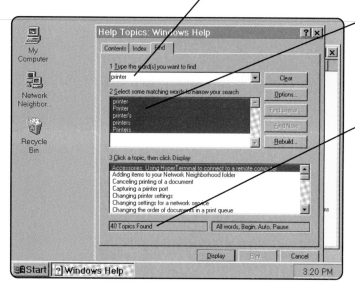

Notice that the highlighted list of words in the Select box has changed to show only variations of the word "printer."

Notice also that the text at the bottom of the dialog box shows the number of topics found that include the five variations of "printer" shown above.

Selecting Matching Words

You can select some or all of the matching words in the middle box for the final search.

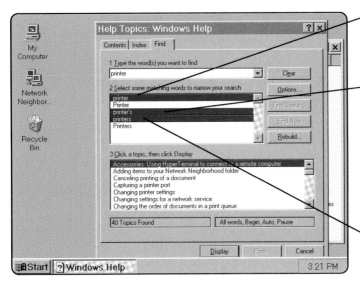

1. Click on **printer** at the top of the list. The word will be highlighted.

2. Press and hold the **Ctrl key**, and then **click** on **printers**, the third word in the list. Holding the Ctrl key while you click allows you to highlight more than one choice in a list.

3. Repeat step 2 to highlight **printers**, the fourth word in the list.

4. Click on the ▼ on the scroll bar to scroll through the list of topics.

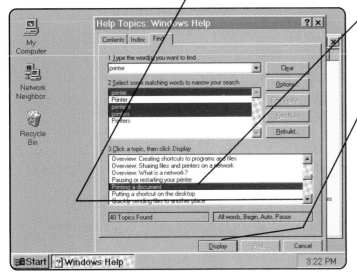

5. Click on the **topic** you want to see to highlight it. In this example, it is Printing a document.

6. Click on **Display**. A window displaying the topic will appear.

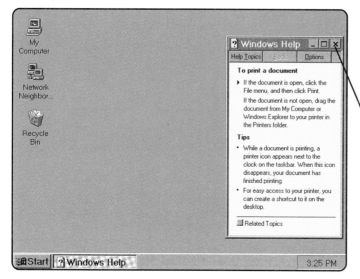

You can do all the things in this Help window that you did in the previous examples in this chapter.

7. **Click** on the **Close button** ([X]) on the right side of the title bar. This will close Help, and you'll be back at the desktop.

Writing a Memo in WordPad

WordPad is a basic word-processing program. In this introduction to WordPad, you will do the following:

✔ Set margins and tabs

✔ Change the font and font style

✔ Enter, edit, and move text

✔ Save, print, and close a file

OPENING WORDPAD

You can use the Start menu to open WordPad as you did in Chapter 1. In this example, you'll use the Run command to open WordPad.

1. Click on the Start button on the taskbar. A pop-up menu will appear (not shown here).

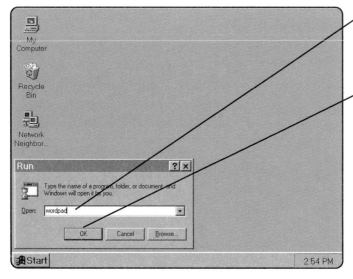

2. **Click** on **Run**. The Run dialog box will appear as you see in this example.

3. **Type wordpad**. It doesn't matter if you type it with capitals or small letters.

4. **Click** on **OK**. After a pause, you'll see an hourglass and a message window, and then WordPad will open.

If the WordPad window does not fill your screen as you see here, click on the Maximize button (□) on the right side of the title bar to maximize the window.

Notice the flashing *insertion point* at the beginning of the document. This shows where the text will be placed when you begin typing.

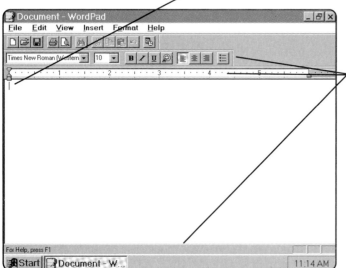

If your WordPad window does not have the bars and the ruler you see here, go to the next section.

TURNING ON THE RULER AND THE BARS

If you don't see a ruler or the two bars at the top of your document, here's how to turn them on.

1. Click on **View** in the menu bar. A menu will appear.

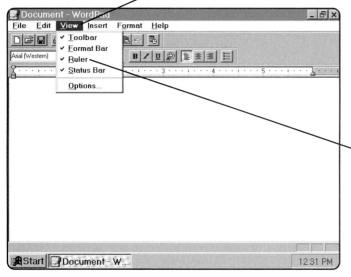

If Ruler, for example, does not have a ✔, you will not have a ruler in the document. (If all the ✔s are there, click anywhere off the menu to close it.)

2. Click on a **missing feature** to insert a ✔. The menu will close. Repeat steps 1 and 2 for each missing item.

CHANGING THE MARGINS

WordPad is set with margins of 1.25 inches on the left and right and 1 inch at the top and bottom. Each of these can be set individually. In this section, you will change the top margin.

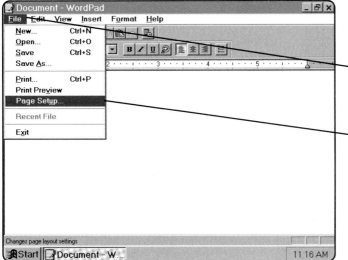

1. **Click** on **File** in the menu bar. A pull-down menu will appear.

2. **Click** on **Page Setup**. The Page Setup dialog box will appear.

Notice that the sample page shows what the printed page will look like with the current margin settings.

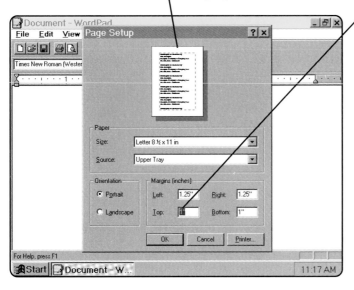

3. **Click twice** on **1"** in the Top box. The number will be highlighted.

4. **Type 2.** It will replace the highlighted number. Notice that the sample letter shows what a 2-inch top margin will look like. This margin will apply to all future documents until you change it.

Instead of closing the dialog box, go on to the next section to find out about portrait and landscape orientation.

CHANGING THE PAPER ORIENTATION

There are two kinds of orientation: portrait and landscape. In this example, you'll compare them.

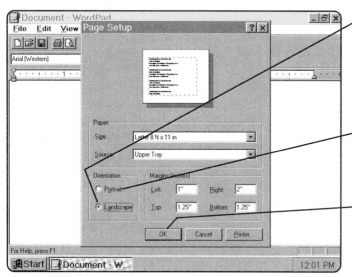

1. **Click** on **Landscape** to put a dot in the circle. Notice that the sample page changes to show how Landscape orientation prints.

2. **Click** on **Portrait** to put a dot in the circle. The sample page will change again.

3. **Click** on **OK** to close the dialog box.

CHANGING THE FONT

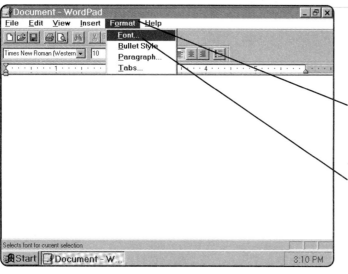

Windows comes with a number of *fonts*, or type styles. In this example, you'll change the font to Arial.

1. **Click** on **Format** in the menu bar. The Format menu will appear.

2. **Click** on **Font**. The Font dialog box will appear.

3. **Place** the mouse arrow on top of the **scroll button**. **Press and hold** the **left mouse button** and **drag** the **scroll button** to the **top** of the **scroll bar**, as you see here. This will take you to the top of the font list.

4. **Click** on **Arial**. Notice that the sample font shows what Arial looks like.

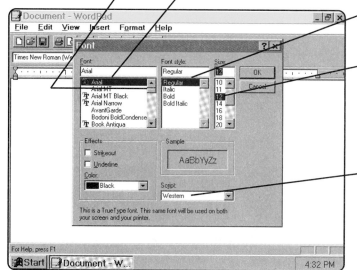

5. **Click** on **Regular** if it is not already highlighted.

6. **Click** on **12**. Most correspondence is typed in 10- or 12-point type. Twelve-point type is a little bigger and easier to read.

Notice that the script is Western.

7. **Click** on **OK** to apply these changes and close the dialog box.

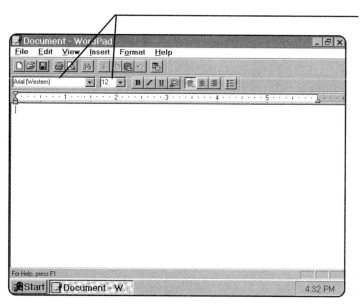

Notice that the formatting toolbar shows that the font is Arial (Western) and the size is 12. Your font may not say "(Western)."

Note: The font change applies only to this document. In a new document, the font will default (go back to) Times New Roman with 10-point type. If you want a different font and size, you must change them again in the new document.

SETTING TABS

When you set tabs before you begin typing, the tabs apply to the entire page until they are changed. If you set a tab in an already typed document, the tab applies only to the paragraph in which it is set. In this section, you'll use two different methods of setting tabs.

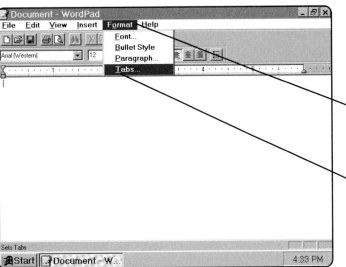

1. **Click** on **Format** in the menu bar. The Format menu will appear.

2. **Click** on **Tabs**. The Tabs dialog box will appear.

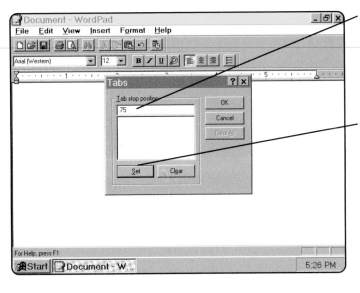

3. **Type .75**. Don't forget the period before the 75 or you'll set the tab at 75 inches instead of at three-quarters of an inch.

4. **Click** on **Set**. You can set additional tabs in this dialog box by repeating steps 3 and 4. In step 6, however, you'll learn a different way to set a tab.

5. **Click** on **OK**. The dialog box will close.

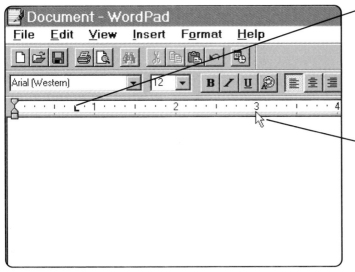

Notice the left tab symbol (L) in the ruler line at the .75-inch mark.

In step 6, you'll learn another way to set a tab.

6. **Point** the mouse arrow at 3 in the ruler and **click** the **left mouse button**. A left tab symbol will appear at the 3-inch mark. Isn't this cool?

REMOVING A TAB

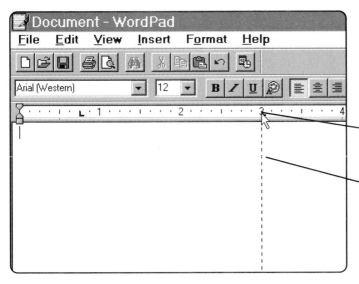

You can remove a tab through the Tab dialog box. In this example, however, you'll use your mouse as a quick and easy method.

1. **Place** the mouse arrow on top of the **tab symbol** at 3".

2. **Press and hold** the mouse button and **drag** the **tab down** into the document. The tab will disappear. Couldn't be easier!

TYPING A MEMO

Now that you have set up the page layout, chosen the font, and set a tab, you are ready to being typing. As with all word-processing programs, you can continue to type without worrying about your right margin. WordPad will bring the text around to the next line automatically.

1. Press the **Caps Lock key** on your keyboard.

2. Type MEMO. You don't have to hold the Shift key because the Caps Lock key is pressed. After a pause, the letters will appear on your screen. If you make a typing error, press the Backspace key to erase the error and type the correct letters.

3. Press the **Caps Lock key** again to turn off the capital letter function.

4. Press the **Enter key twice** to insert a double space after MEMO.

5. Type To: and **press** the **Tab key**. The cursor will move to the tab you set earlier.

6. Type Carolyn Holder and **press** the **Enter key twice**.

7. Type From: and **press** the **Tab key**.

8. Type Maura Healy and **press** the **Enter key twice**.

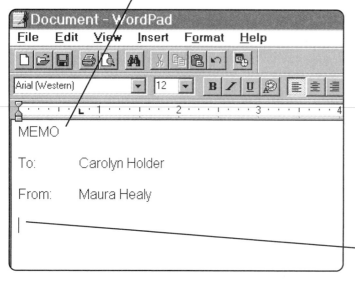

Inserting the Date

You can, of course, type the date. However, WordPad has a button that will insert it for you.

1. **Type Date:** and **press** the **Tab key**.

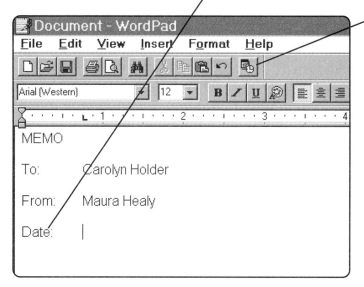

2. **Click** on the **Date/Time button** in the toolbar. The Date and Time dialog box will appear.

3. **Click** on the ▼ to scroll through the list until you see a form of the date and/or time that you like.

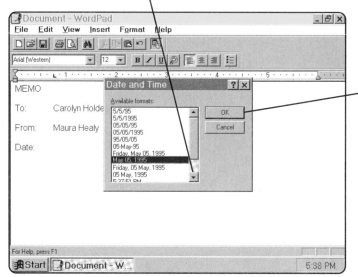

4. **Click** on the form you like. In this example, it is **May 05, 1995**.

5. **Click** on **OK** to close the dialog box. The date will appear in the memo at the cursor.

6. **Press** the **Enter key twice** to insert a double space after the date.

COMPLETING THE MEMO

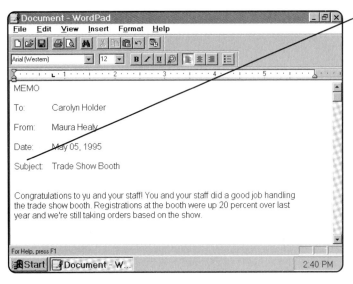

1. **Type** the **subject line** you see here.

2. **Press** the **Enter key three times**.

3. **Type** the **text** you see in this example. The text contains an error that you will correct later in this chapter, so include it if you want to follow along with these procedures. In word processing, you press the spacebar *only once* after a period.

EDITING TEXT

This section will cover basic editing procedures. These procedures apply to all Windows programs.

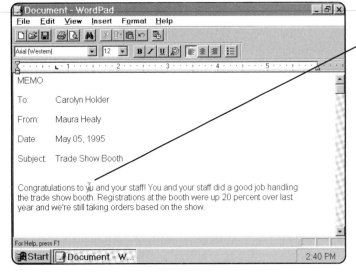

Inserting Text

1. **Place** the mouse pointer **between** the letters **y** and **u**. The pointer will be in the shape of an I-beam.

2. **Click** to set the cursor in place.

3. **Type** the letter **o**. It will be inserted into the word. You can insert letters, words, and even entire paragraphs this way.

Deleting Text

In this section, you'll delete the words "at the booth."

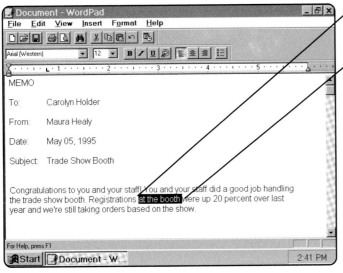

1. **Click** at the beginning of "at" to place the cursor.

2. **Press and hold** the mouse button and **drag** the cursor over "**at the booth.**" The words and the space at the end will be highlighted.

3. **Press** the **Delete key** on your keyboard. The highlighted words will be deleted.

Changing Text

In this section, you'll change the word "good" to "terrific."

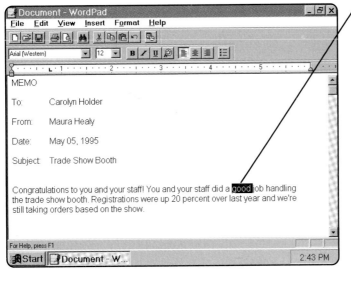

1. **Click twice** on **good**. The word and the space after it will be highlighted.

2. **Type** the word **terrific**. "Terrific" will replace "good."

MOVING TEXT

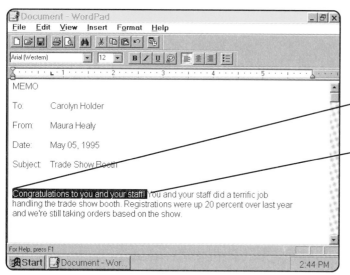

In this section, you'll cut a piece of text from one part of the memo and paste it into another part.

1. Click to the **left** of the **first sentence** to place the cursor.

2. Press and hold the **mouse button** and **drag** the cursor to the **end of the sentence** to highlight it. Notice that the highlight bar automatically includes the space after the sentence.

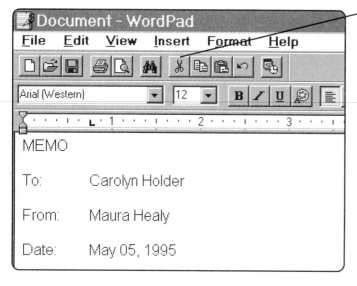

3. Click on the **Cut button** (the scissors) in the toolbar. After a pause, the highlighted sentence will be cut from the text.

4. Click at the **end** of the memo to place the cursor. **Press** the **Enter key twice** to put a double space after the last sentence.

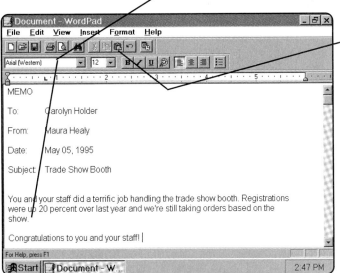

5. Click on the **Paste button** (the clipboard). It's the third button from the right in the top toolbar. The text you cut from the beginning of the memo will be pasted into the memo at the cursor, as you see here.

CENTERING TEXT

In this section, you'll center the line "Congratulations to you and your staff!"

1. Place the mouse arrow in the **left margin** beside the last sentence and click twice to highlight the entire line. The screen may "jump up" a line.

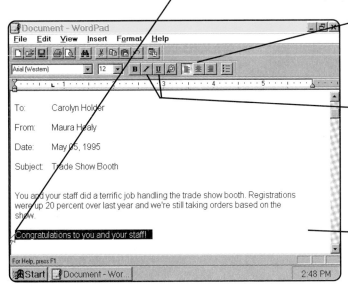

2. Click on the **Center button**. The highlighted text will be centered across the page.

3. While the text is highlighted, **click** on the **Underline** (<u>U</u>) and **Italic** (*I*) buttons to see what they do. Then click again to turn each function off.

4. Click on a **clear space** to remove the highlighting.

CHANGING FONT SIZE

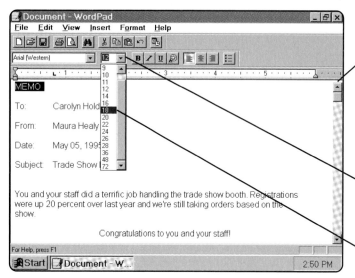

In this section, you'll increase the size of MEMO.

1. Click on the ▲ to take you to the top of the file.

2. Click twice in the **left margin** beside MEMO to highlight it.

3. Click on the ▼ to the right of the Font Size box. A menu will appear.

4. Click on **18**. The highlighted text will change to 18-point type.

MAKING TEXT BOLD

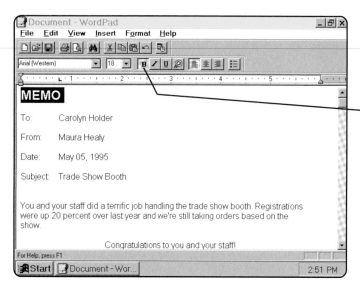

In this example, you'll make MEMO boldfaced. The text should be highlighted, as it is in this example.

1. While the text is highlighted, **click** on the **Bold button (B)**. The highlighted text will become bold. The Bold button works like a switch. Click again to turn it off.

2. Click anywhere to remove the highlighting.

NAMING AND SAVING THE MEMO

In Windows 95, you can have long filenames (up to 255 characters, including spaces). You cannot, however, use the following characters: \ ? : * " < > x.

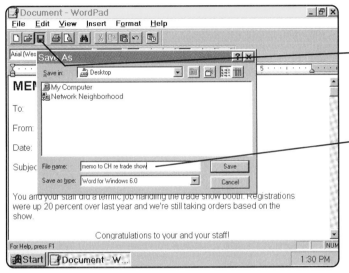

1. Click on the **Save button**. It's the third from the left. The Save As dialog box you see here will appear.

2. Type the **name** you want to give the file. It will replace "Document" in the File name box.

When you save a file, you first have to select a folder to put it in.

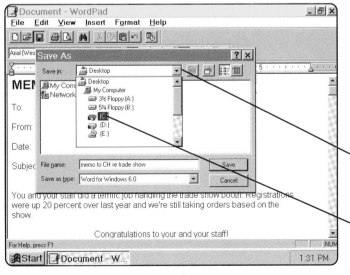

Currently, the file will be saved to the desktop, meaning that it will appear on the opening screen of Windows 95. In this example, you'll choose a folder to put it in.

3 Click on the ▼ to the right of the Save in box to show a list of drives.

4. Click on **(C:)**. A list of the folders on the C: drive will appear.

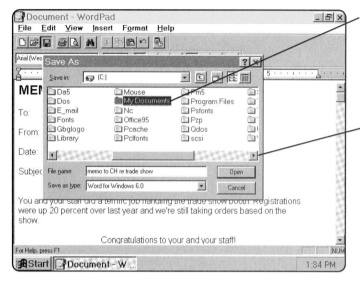

5. Click twice on **My Documents**. This is a folder that Windows 95 created when it was installed on your computer.

If you don't see My Documents, click on the ▶ until you can see it.

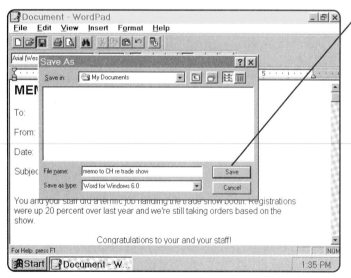

6. Click on **Save**. The memo (which is officially called a *file* or a *document*) will be saved.

Notice that the name of the file is now in the title bar.

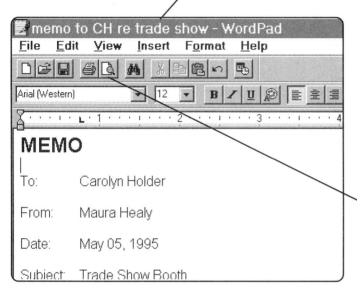

PRINTING THE MEMO

You can print by clicking on the Print button in the tool-bar. It's the fourth button from the left. However, in this example, you'll go to Print Preview first.

1. Click on the **Print Preview button**. It's the fifth button in the toolbar. After a pause, the Print Preview screen will appear.

The Print Preview screen shows you what the document looks like on the page.

2. Click on **Print**. The Print dialog box will appear.

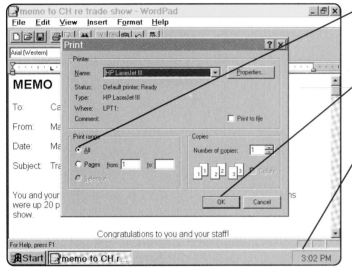

3. Click on **All** to put a dot in the circle if one is not already there.

4. Click on **OK**. A message box will appear, telling you that the file is printing.

When the message box disappears, a little printer will appear on the time button on the taskbar.

CLOSING WORDPAD

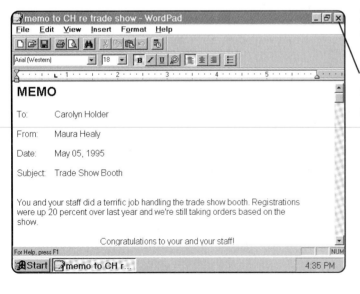

In this example, you'll close the memo and WordPad.

1. Click on the **Close button** ([**X**]) in the title bar. WordPad and the memo will close.

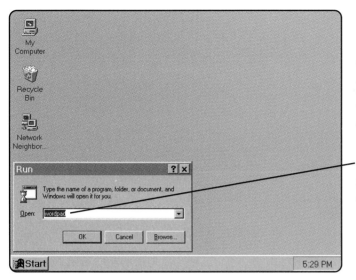

OPENING A SAVED FILE

In this section, you'll open the memo you wrote to Carolyn Holder.

1. **Open WordPad**. See the first few steps in Chapter 9 to use the Run command.

2. **Click** on **File** in the menu bar. The File menu will appear.

Notice that the memo to CH is on the menu. The File menu lists the most recently opened files. If others have used WordPad, there may be other files listed on this menu. If you saved your file with a different name, the filename may show as C:\MyDocuments\ filename.

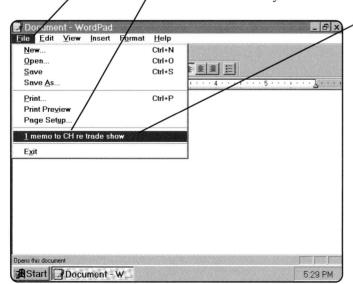

3. **Click** on the **file** you want to open. It will appear on your screen. You can then edit the file as you did in this chapter.

This introduction to WordPad was designed to give you the confidence to experiment with WordPad's other features. WordPad files can be used in Word for Windows and other word-processing programs.

Playing Games

No computer user worthy of his or her mouse would leave the Games package untouched and languishing on the hard drive. Playing games is one of the time-honored traditions of using a computer. Windows 95 comes with five games. In this chapter, you will do the following:

✔ Open a game
✔ Learn about Solitaire

OPENING A GAME

You get to the games through the Start menu.

1. **Click** on the **Start button** on the taskbar. A pop-up menu will appear.

2. **Move** the mouse arrow up to **Programs** to highlight it. Another menu will appear.

3. **Move** the mouse arrow to **Accessories**. The Accessories menu will appear.

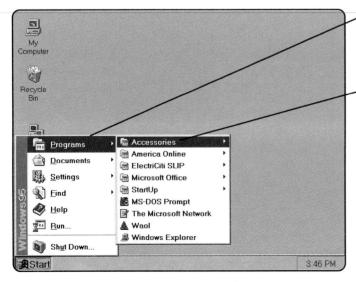

Windows 95

Programs   ▶   Accessories   ▶
Documents   ▶   America Online   ▶
Settings   ▶   ElectriCiti SLIP   ▶
Find   ▶   Microsoft Office   ▶
Help   StartUp   ▶
Run...   MS-DOS Prompt
Shut Down...   The Microsoft Network
    Waol
    Windows Explorer

My Computer
Recycle Bin

Start   3:46 PM

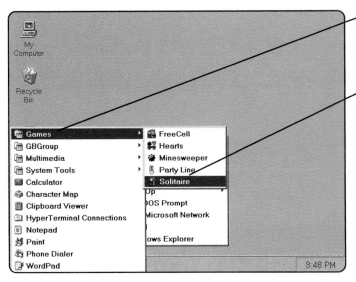

4. **Move** the mouse arrow to **Games**. The Games menu will appear.

5. **Click** on **Solitaire**. After a pause, the Solitaire window you see in the next example will appear.

LEARNING TO PLAY SOLITAIRE

You can use Help to get a copy of the rules and scoring for each of the five games that comes with Windows. The following steps apply to any game, not just Solitaire.

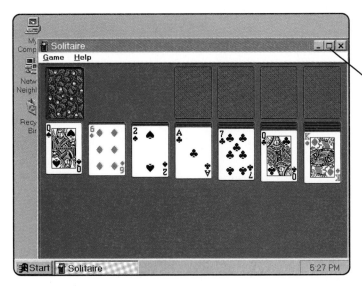

1. **Click** on the **Maximize button** (□) to make the Solitaire window fill the screen.

2. Click on **Help** in the menu bar. A pull-down menu will appear.

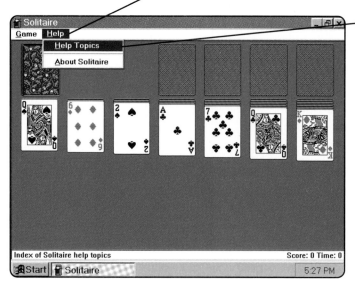

3. Click on **Help Topics**. The Help Topics: Solitaire Help window will appear. The first time you open a Help topic, you'll see a graphic of a pen writing in a book as Windows builds the topic.

Note: If you upgraded from Windows 3.1, you may see additional choices on the Help menu. Click on Contents. The Contents window will be a little different from the one you see in the next example. You may have to click on a choice about rules.

4. Click twice on **How to play Solitaire**. A Help window will appear with this topic displayed. If you haven't used Help before, you may want to refer to Chapter 11, "Exploring Help," for more details.

Printing the Rules

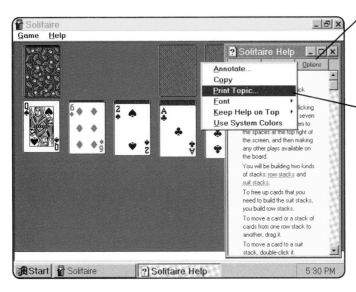

1. **Click** on **Options** in the Help window. The pop-up menu you see here will appear.

2. **Click** on **Print Topic**. After a pause, the text will print.

3. **Click** on the **Help Topics button** (underneath the pop-up menu in this picture) to go back to the original Help window.

4. **Repeat step 4** in the previous section and **steps 1 and 2** above to print the scoring information.

5. **Click** on the **Close button** (⨯) to close the Help window when you're through.

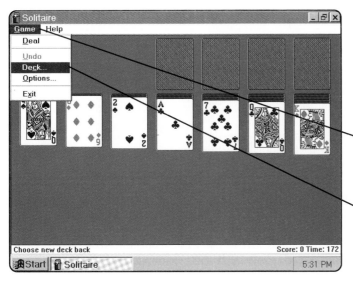

CHANGING THE DECK

You can change the appearance of the deck.

1. **Click** on **Game** in the menu bar. A pull-down menu will appear.

2. **Click** on **Deck**. The Select Card Back window will appear.

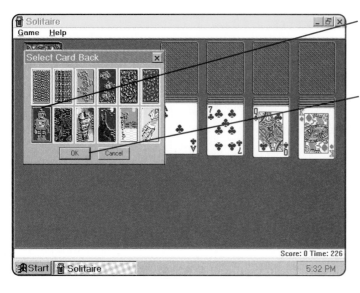

3. Click on the **design** you want to see on the cards. In this example, it's the robot.

4. Click on **OK**. The window will close.

DEALING A NEW GAME AND CHANGING THE SCORING

You can deal a new game at any time.

1. Click on **Game** in the menu bar. A pull-down menu will appear.

2. Click on **Deal**. You'll be dealt a new setup.

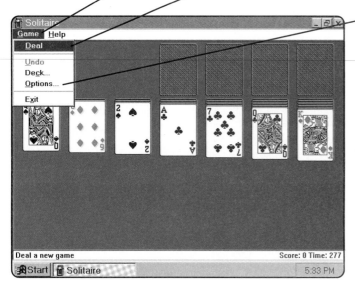

3. Repeat step 1 and **click on Options** on the Game menu. A dialog box will appear that allows you to choose a different scoring method (not shown here). You can also click on Help in the menu bar to learn about scoring.

Notice also that there is an Undo option on this menu that will undo a move.

Have fun with the games! They can be addicting.

Exploring the Three Cs

If you're one of those people who like to keep things organized, you'll like Windows 95's calculator, calendar, and cardfile for handling some of your basic tasks. Microsoft used the "KISS" method in designing these programs. They are very simple and straightforward. In this chapter, you will do the following:

✔ Preview the calculator

✔ Explore the calendar

✔ Enter a name in the cardfile

PREVIEWING THE CALCULATOR

In this section you will view the calculator in its standard and scientific views.

1. **Click** on **Start**. A menu will appear.

2. **Click** on **Programs**. A menu will appear.

3. **Move** the mouse arrow to **Accessories**. A menu will appear.

4. **Click** on **Calculator**. The calculator will appear.

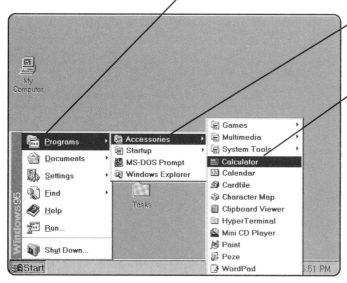

❶ This operates like a regular desktop calculator. Click on the number and functions buttons, and the results appear in the numbers text box.

❷ When you click on Edit in the menu bar, a pull-down menu will appear with the option to copy your "numbers" after you have completed your calculation.

5. **Click** on **View** in the menu bar. A menu will appear.

6. **Click** on **Scientific**. The scientific calculator will appear.

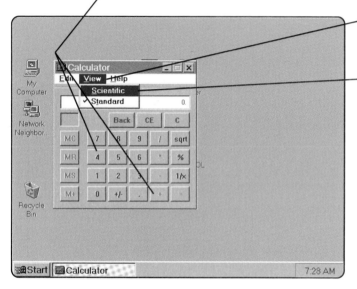

Mmmmm. This looks complicated, but no doubt engineers will like it!

7. **Click** on the **Close button** (☒) in the right corner of the title bar to close the program.

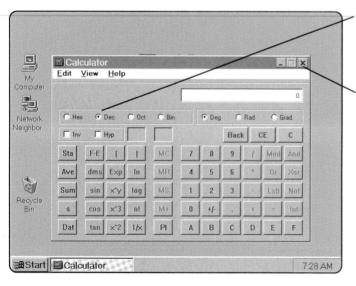

EXPLORING THE CALENDAR

In this section, you will enter an appointment and set an alarm for it. Next, you will save the calendar, print your appointments, close the calendar, and reopen it.

1. Repeat steps 1 through 4 in the previous section, but this time open the calendar.

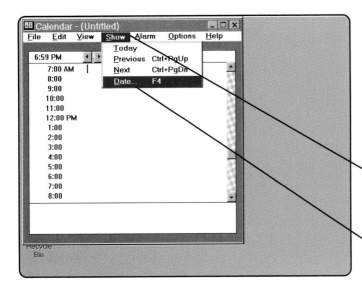

MAKING AN APPOINTMENT

In this section, you will make an appointment for a future date.

1. Click on **Show** in the menu bar. The Show menu will appear.

2. Click on **Date**. The Show Date dialog box will appear.

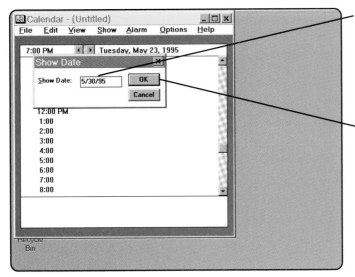

3. Type the **date** of the appointment, as shown here. You must use this particular format. Typing "May 30, 1995" won't work.

4. Click on **OK**. The calendar for the date you typed will appear.

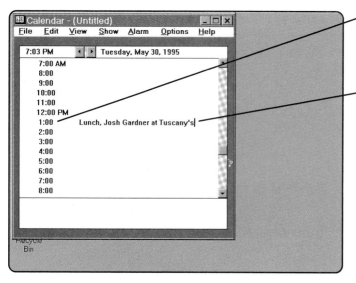

5. Click to the **right** of the time you want to schedule to set the cursor.

6. Type the **appointment information**. You can basically type anything here.

Setting An Alarm

It's always a good idea to set an alarm for an appointment.

1. Click on **Alarm**. A menu will appear.

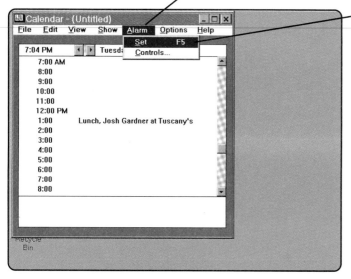

2. Click on **Set**. A little bell will appear to the left of the appointment.

Note: You can set the alarm to go off earlier than the appointment time (not shown here). Just click on Alarm, click on Controls and then type the number of minutes you want the alarm to go off before the actual appointment in the early ring box (1 to 10 minutes).

Notice the little bell!

Talking About Views . . .

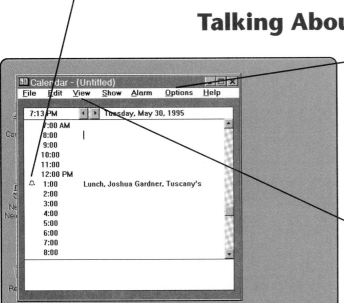

❶ You can change the time interval to every 15 minutes or to every 30 minutes. Simply click on Options and then on Day Settings. Next click on the interval you want to put a dot in the circle and click on OK.

❷ You can view the month-at-a-glance by simply clicking on View and then clicking on Month. Unfortunately, none of the appointments will show.

Saving the Calendar

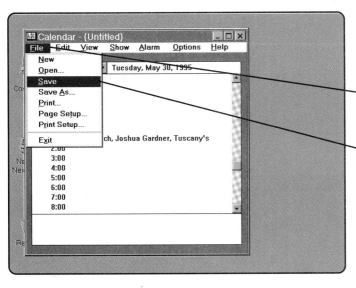

You can make as many calendars as you like. In this case, one is enough.

1. **Click** on **File** in the menu bar. A menu will appear.

2. **Click** on **Save**. The Save As dialog box will appear.

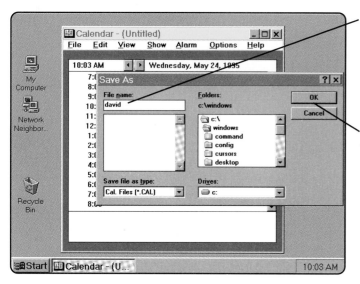

3. **Type** a **name** for the calendar file. (For you folks who are interested, calendar will automatically put in the .cal extension.)

4. **Click** on **OK**. The dialog box will close.

Printing Appointments

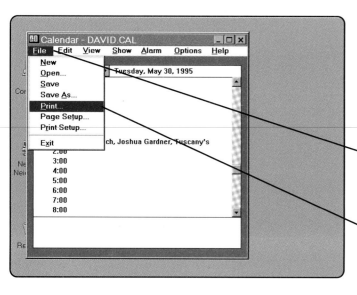

It's a good idea to print your appointments daily (or weekly) since you cannot view your appointments for the month in the monthly view.

1. **Click** on **File** in the menu bar. The File menu will appear.

2. **Click** on **Print**. The Print dialog box will appear.

Notice that the date in the From box matches the date in the calendar.

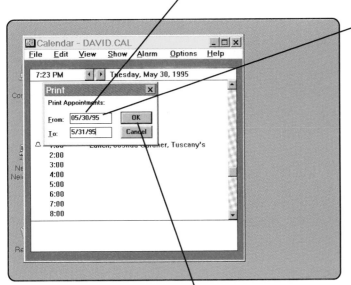

3. **Type** a **new From date** if you want to change the highlighted date currently there.

4. If you want to change the To date, **click twice** in the **To box** to highlight the date that is there. **Type** a **new date**. In this example, we did not change the From date, and we entered the next day into the To date. This will print appointments for two days.

5. **Click** on **OK**. The list of appointments for the specified dates will print.

Closing the Calendar

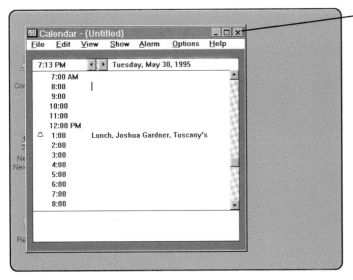

1. **Click** on the **Close button** (⊠) in the right corner of the title bar to close the program.

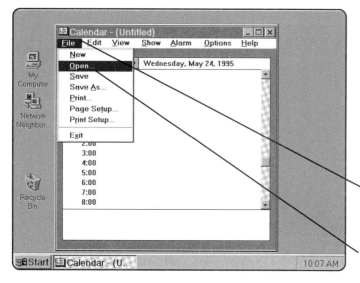

Opening Your Calendar

The next time you open the calendar, an untitled calendar appears. To get to your saved calendar, follow the steps below.

1. **Click** on **File** in the menu bar. The File menu will appear.

2. **Click** on **Open**. The Open dialog box will appear.

3. **Click** on the **name** of your calendar.

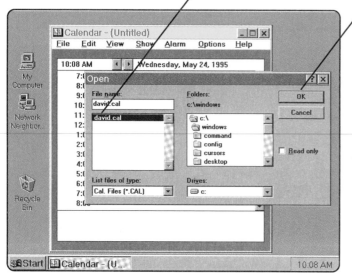

4. **Click** on **OK**. The calendar you saved in the previous section will open. Close the calendar at any time by clicking on the Close button (X).

✔ **Tip:** If you are going to use the calendar regularly, create a shortcut icon for it and put it on the desktop. See Chapter 10, the section entitled "Putting a Document Icon on the Desktop." Your calendar will always be available with just two clicks of the mouse!

ENTERING NAMES IN THE CARDFILE

In this section, you will enter names into the cardfile and save them.

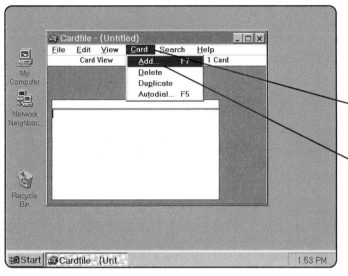

1. **Repeat steps 1 through 4** on the first page of this chapter, but this time open the cardfile, as shown here.

2. **Click** on **Card** in the menu bar. A menu will appear.

3. **Click** on **Add**. The Add dialog box will appear.

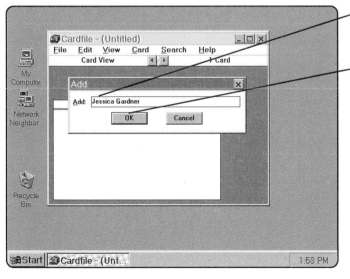

4. **Type** a **name** in the Add text box.

5. **Click** on **OK**. A new, blank card with the person's name in the title bar will appear.

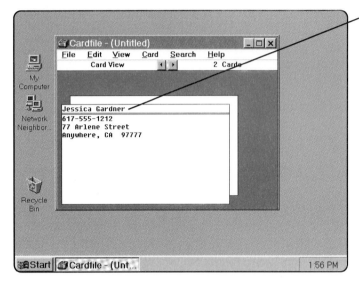

6. **Type** the **phone number**, **address**, and any **other information** you want to keep on the individual's card.

7. **Repeat steps 2 through 6** to create as many cards as you like.

8. **Repeat steps 1 through 3** in the section entitled "Saving the Calendar" to save the card file. Close the Cardfile at any time by clicking on the Close button ([×]).

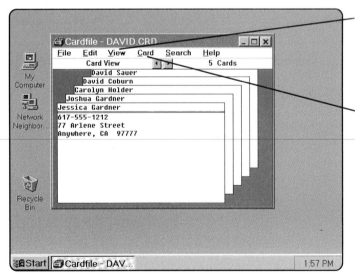

❶ You can view the cards like this or you can view them as a list by clicking on View and then clicking on List.

❷ You can dial a phone number (if you have a modem and if you have a telephone attached to your computer) by highlighting the number and clicking on Card, then Autodial, then OK, and finally on OK after the telephone rings.

✔ **Tip:** If you are going to use the Cardfile regularly, create a shortcut icon for it and put it on the desktop. See Chapter 10, the section entitled "Putting a Document Icon on the Desktop." Your cardfile will always be available with just two clicks of the mouse!

Becoming a Computer Picasso

Windows has a drawing program called Paint. Although it's not a sophisticated program, you can create exciting pictures and have a lot of fun with it. You can even import your artwork into your word processing program. In this introduction to Paint, you will do the following:

✔ Create various shapes and text
✔ Use Edit Undo
✔ Erase lines
✔ Color your drawing
✔ Save the drawing and import it into WordPad

OPENING THE PAINT PROGRAM

Paint is in the Accessories group of programs.

1. Click on the **Start button** on the taskbar. A pop-up menu will appear.

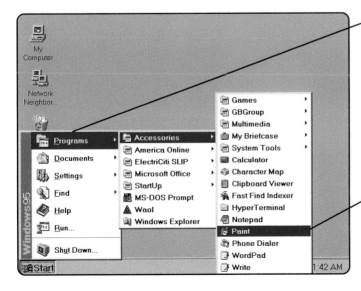

2. Move the mouse arrow to **Programs**. Another menu will appear.

3. Move the mouse arrow to **Accessories**. A third menu will appear. It may appear in a different spot than you see here.

4. Click on **Paint**. The untitled - Paint window will appear.

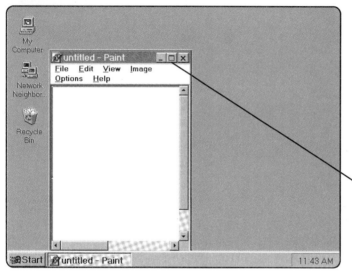

Your Paint window may appear in a different size and in a different spot from the one you see here.

If the window does not fill your screen, you can maximize the window.

5. Click on the **Maximize button** (□) on the right side of the Paint title bar.

LINING UP YOUR TOOLS

As you get ready to create your masterpiece, it helps to have all your tools available. Paint comes with several special tool boxes.

1. Click on **View** in the menu bar. The View menu will appear.

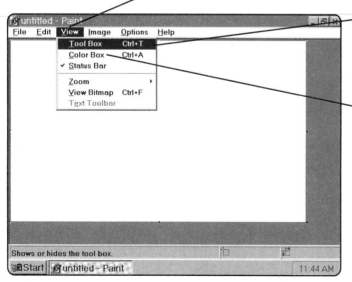

2. Click on **Tool Box** if a ✔ is not already there. The menu will close, and the tool box will appear on your screen.

3. Repeat step 1 to open the View menu, and click on Color Box if it is not already ✔'d.

Your goal in this chapter is to create a drawing like the one at the bottom of page 164. Relax and have fun!

DRAWING CIRCLES

1. Click on the **Ellipse tool** in the tool box. It will appear pressed in. (Notice that a label for the Ellipse tool appears if you rest the mouse arrow on the tool. Try pointing at other tools to see the names.)

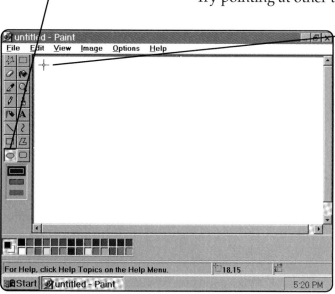

2. Place the mouse pointer in the **upper-left corner** of the screen. Notice that the pointer has changed to the shape you see here.

3. Press and hold the mouse button and **drag** the pointer **down and** to the **right** to form a circle. Notice that you can adjust the shape as long as you continue to hold the mouse button.

4. Release the **button** when the circle is the shape you want.

5. Repeat steps 2 through 4 to make a second circle similar to what you see here.

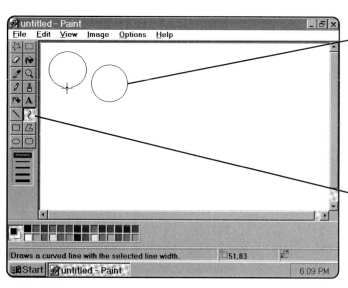

DRAWING CURVED LINES

1. Click on the **Curve tool**, and **place** the **pointer** at the bottom of the first circle where you see the plus sign in this example.

2. Press and hold the mouse button, and **drag** the pointer **down** to form a straight line, then **release** the mouse button.

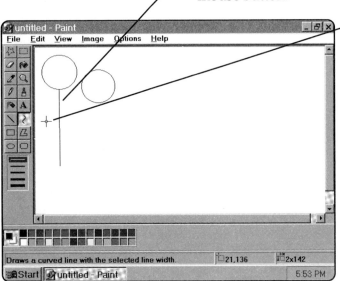

3. Place the mouse pointer to the **left of the line**, as you see here.

4. Click twice and watch what happens! The line will curve in proportion to how far away from the line you place the mouse pointer when you click. (Instead of clicking the second time in the same place, you can change the position of the pointer for the second click. When you click the second time, it will put a second curve into the line.

UNDOING A MOVE

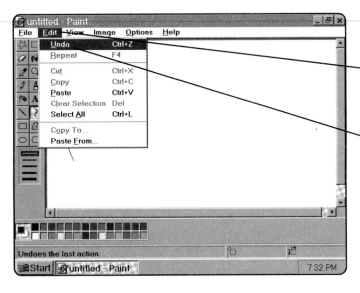

You can use the Edit menu to undo up to three moves.

1. Click on **Edit** in the menu bar. The Edit menu will appear.

2. Click on **Undo**. This will remove the last move you made. You can undo the last three moves by repeating steps 1 and 2. After three times, the Undo option will be grayed out, meaning that it is not available at this time.

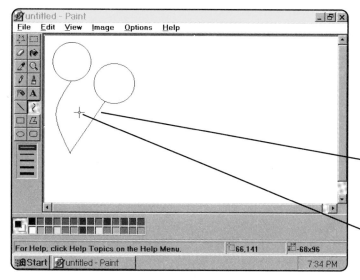

FINISHING THE BALLOONS

1. Repeat the **steps** in the previous sections to make the two balloons you see here.

2. Draw the **line** for the second balloon as you see here.

3. Place the mouse pointer to the **left** of the second line, and click twice to curve the line.

SAVING AND PRINTING YOUR WORK

We recommend that you save your work *often!* Develop the habit of saving often, and you'll save yourself much grief and aggravation.

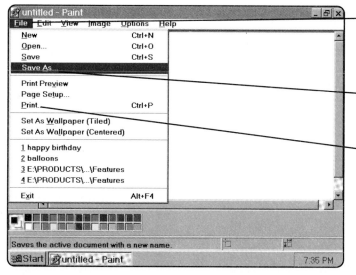

1. Click on **File** in the menu bar. The File menu will appear.

2. Click on **Save As**. The Save As dialog box will appear.

(After you finish step 4, come back here and **click** on **Print** to print your artwork.)

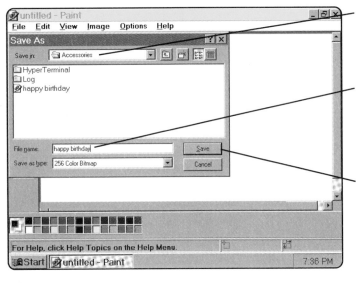

Notice that the file will be saved in the Accessories folder.

3. Type happy birthday (which is the name we will give this file) in the File name box.

4. Click on **Save**. The Save As dialog box will close, and the file is now saved.

DRAWING RECTANGLES

1. Click on the **Rectangle tool** in the tool box.

2. Place the mouse pointer at **approximately this point**. **Press and hold** the mouse button and **drag** the pointer **down and** to the **right** to form a narrow rectangle. **Release** the mouse pointer.

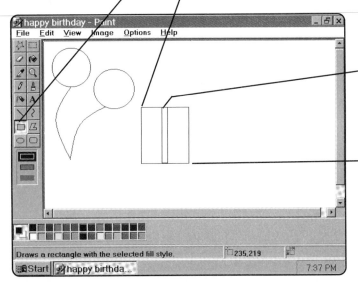

Now you'll draw a second, overlapping rectangle.

3. Place the mouse pointer on the **top line** of the first rectangle, about ½ inch inside the right edge.

4. Press and hold the mouse button and **drag** to draw a second rectangle. **Release** the mouse button.

5. Click on **File** in the menu bar, and then **click** on **Save**.

DRAWING LINES

In this example, you'll put a "bow" on the top of the "present."

1. **Click** on the **Line tool** in the tool box.

2. **Place** the mouse pointer on the top of the present.

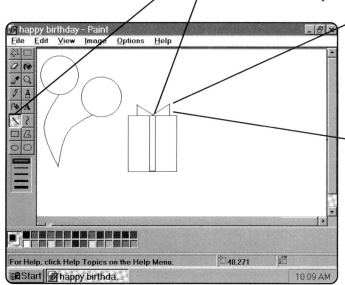

3. **Press and hold** the mouse button, and **drag** the pointer **up and** to the **right** to make a diagonal line.

4. **Release** the mouse button.

5. **Press and hold** the mouse button, and **drag** the pointer **down** to make a straight line, then **release** the mouse button.

6. **Repeat steps 2 through 5** to make the "bow" on the other side.

ZOOMING IN

1. **Click** on **View** in the menu bar. The View menu will appear.

2. **Move** the mouse arrow to **Zoom**.

3. **Click** on **Large Size** to zoom in for a close-up.

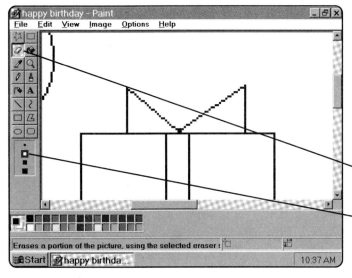

ERASING

In this section, you'll use the eraser instead of Undo.

1. **Click** on the ▼ and ▶ on the scroll bars until you see the view you see here.

2. **Click** on the **Eraser/Color** Eraser in the tool box.

3. **Click** on the **second eraser head** in the size list. The pointer will change to a square.

4. **Place** the **square** on the line you want to erase. Be careful with the placement. Notice in this example that the eraser outline is placed just above the top line of the present.

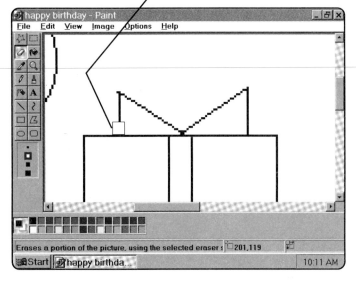

5. **Click** the **mouse button**. The area under the eraser head will be erased.

Note: You can erase one small area at a time by placing the eraser and then clicking. Or you can press and hold the mouse button and drag the eraser over a wide area. Be very careful because the eraser will erase *anything* it touches.

6. Erase the **left half** of the **bow**.

COPYING A PART OF THE DRAWING

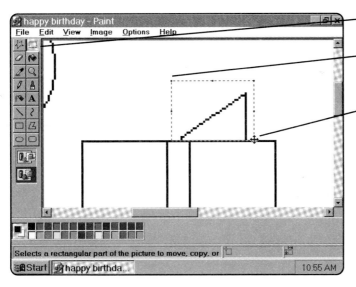

1. **Click** on the **Select tool**.

2. **Place** the mouse pointer at **approximately this spot**.

3. **Press and hold** the mouse button, and **drag** the pointer and the resulting dotted box around the triangle as you see here.

4. **Release** the mouse button when the dotted box surrounds the triangle.

5. **Click** on **Edit** in the menu bar. The Edit menu will appear.

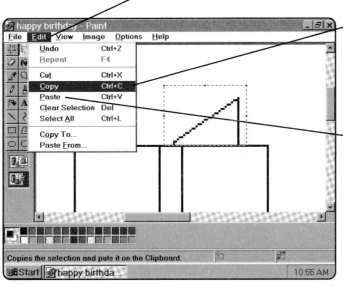

6. **Click** on **Copy**. You won't see any difference in your screen, but the selected area is now copied to the Clipboard.

7. **Repeat step 5** and **click** on **Paste**. After a pause, a copy of the selected area will be pasted into the picture. It may appear in the upper left corner of your screen.

8. Place the mouse pointer on **top** of the new triangle, and then **press and hold** the mouse button and drag the triangle to the **top** of the **present**. It may move a little awkwardly, but have patience and keep at it until it is in the right spot. You may have to release the mouse button, see where it is positioned, and then move it again.

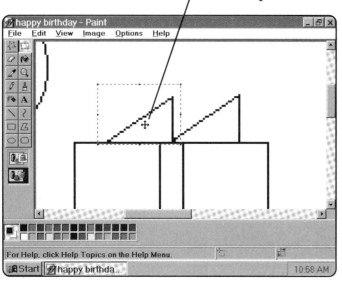

You'll notice, of course, that the left bow is backward. No problem: You'll fix it in the next section.

ROTATING AN IMAGE

1. While the triangle still has the dotted box around it, **click** on **Image** in the menu bar. The Image menu will appear.

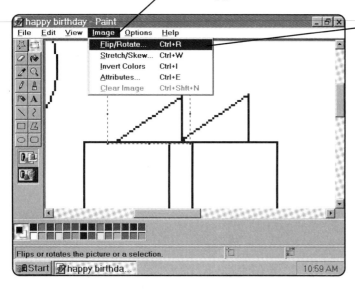

2. Click on **Flip/Rotate**. The Flip and Rotate dialog box will appear.

3. Click on **Flip horizontal** to put a dot in the circle if one is not already there. This will flip the image right to left.

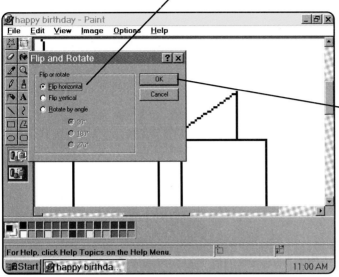

If you click on Flip vertical, it will flip the image top to bottom.

4. Click on **OK**. The image will be flipped and the "bow" will be complete.

5. Repeat the **steps** in "Zooming In" and **click** on **Normal Size**. Click on the scroll bar arrows to get back to the view you see in the next example.

ADDING TEXT

Before you can type text, you must add a *text block* to hold the text.

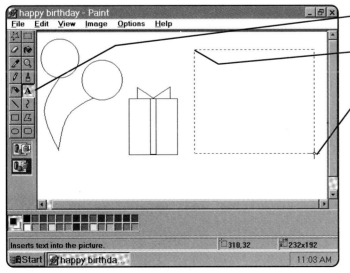

1. Click on the **Text tool**.

2. Place the mouse pointer at **approximately this spot**.

3. Press and hold the mouse button, and drag to form a dotted box, as you see here.

4. Release the mouse button when the box is about as large as the one in this example.

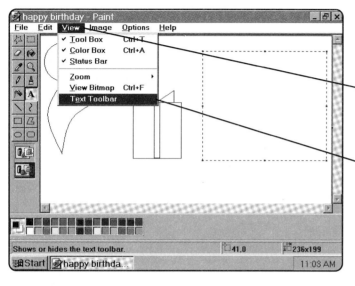

Showing the Text Toolbar

1. Click on **View** in the menu bar. The View menu will appear.

2. Click on **Text Toolbar**. The menu will close, and the text toolbar will appear on your screen. From now on, when you draw a text box, the text toolbar will appear.

3. Click on the ▼ to the right of the Font box. A list of fonts will appear (not shown here). Click on the font you want. In this example, we've chosen Arial (Western).

4. Click on the ▼ to the right of the Size box. A list of sizes will appear.

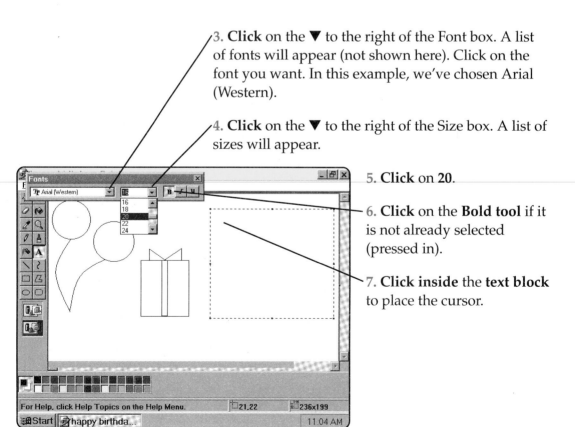

5. Click on **20**.

6. Click on the **Bold tool** if it is not already selected (pressed in).

7. Click inside the **text block** to place the cursor.

Typing Text

Now that the text block has been added and you've chosen your font and the font size and style, you're ready to type the text.

1. **Type** the **message**. The text will automatically wrap to the next line when it reaches the end of the text block. In this example, press the Enter key twice after each line to deliberately put the text on a separate line and to insert a blank line after the text.

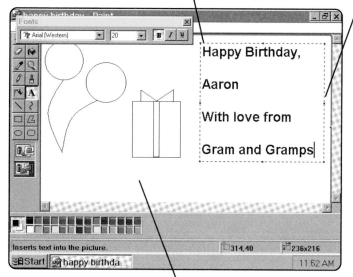

For future work, you should know that you can expand the text block by putting the mouse arrow on top of the mark in the middle of the text block. The mouse arrow will change into a two-headed arrow. Drag the text block to the right to expand it. (You can't do that here because there is no room to expand to the right.)

As long as this text block is active (the border is still around it), you can edit the text. After you do step 2, you cannot change the text.

2. **Click anywhere** on the page to remove the border from the text block. The Text Toolbar will disappear, and the text is now permanent. To change the text, erase it or use the Select tool to surround it, and then use Cut on the Edit menu to cut it out of the page.

3. **Click** on **File** in the menu bar, and then **click** on **Save** on the File menu to save all this work.

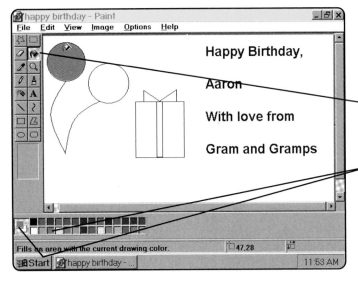

ADDING COLOR

Now comes the really fun part!

1. **Click** on the **Fill with Color tool**. It looks like a paint can spilling paint.

2. **Click** on the **red square** in the color box. Notice that the sample color turns red.

3. **Place** the **paint can inside** the **first balloon** and **press** the **mouse button**. The circle will be filled with red. Isn't this cool?!

4. **Repeat step 2** to choose a different color and color the second balloon.

5. **Continue to repeat step 2** to change colors and **paint** each part of the **picture**.

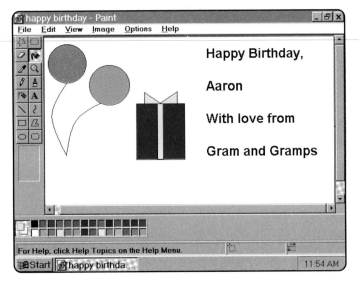

Note A: Sometimes the paint can spills color on the entire picture instead of on the little part you want to color. Just use Undo and try again. You may have to try several times to color just the bow.

Note B: Change back to black to draw or else your lines will be the last color you chose.

6. **Be sure to save**.

IMPORTING YOUR ARTWORK INTO WORDPAD

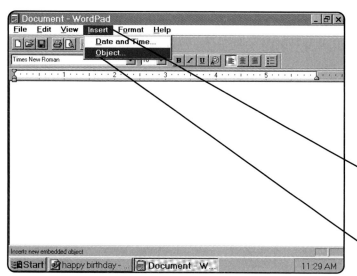

You don't have to close Paint in order to go to WordPad.

1. Use the Start button on the taskbar to open WordPad. See Chapter 1 if you need help.

2. Click on **Insert** in the menu bar. The Insert menu will appear.

3. Click on **Object**. A dialog box will appear.

4. Click on **Create from File** to put a dot in the circle. Normally, you click on Browse to go through a series of dialog boxes to get to the file. We'll teach you a shortcut.

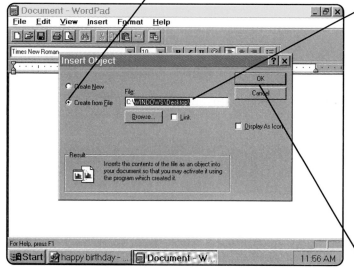

5. Click at the **end of the text** to place the cursor.

6. Press and hold the mouse button and **drag** the highlight bar **over the text**. Don't highlight the C:\ at the beginning of the text.

7. Type program files\ accessories\happy birthday (in one line). This is called the *path*, or address, of the file.

8. Click on **OK**.

After a pause, your artwork will appear.

Sizing the Artwork

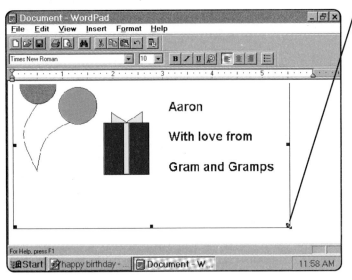

1. Place the mouse pointer on the **black square** in the lower right corner of the picture. The pointer will change into a two-headed arrow.

2. Press and hold the mouse button and drag the **corner** of the picture **up and** to the **left** to reduce the picture proportionally.

3. Release the mouse button when the picture is the size you want.

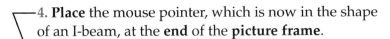

4. Place the mouse pointer, which is now in the shape of an I-beam, at the **end** of the **picture frame**.

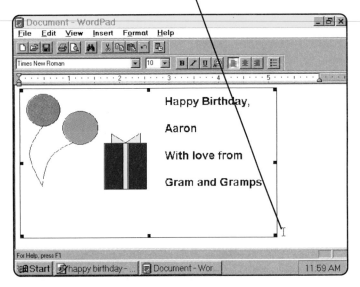

5. Click the **mouse button**, and the picture frame will disappear.

6. Press the **spacebar** on your keyboard to move the I-beam below the picture. Now you can start typing regular text in WordPad.

Follow the standard procedures to save this file, and then close WordPad and Paint.

Have fun with Paint!

WINDOWS 95

Seeing What's on Your Computer

The files and programs on your computer are organized into folders, just like the information in a filing cabinet. You can create new folders, move information from one folder to another, and throw away, or delete, old folders just like you do in your filing cabinet. You can even check to see how much free storage space you have on your computer. One of the ways to do this in Windows 95 is with the My Computer icon on your desktop. Windows 95 also gives you a very easy way to search for a file if you've forgotten where you put it. In this chapter, you will do the following:

✔ See what's on your C: drive

✔ Make and name a new folder

✔ Learn two ways to move a file between folders

✔ Delete a folder

✔ Check disk space

✔ Find a file

OPENING MY COMPUTER

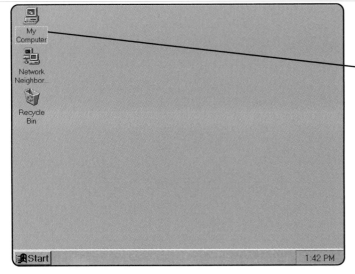

My Computer shows you what is on your computer.

1. **Click twice** on **My Computer**. A window called My Computer will appear.

The A: drive on your computer is the small slot that is in the tower or box. This is the slot in which you put disks that are approximately 3½ inches square. The label shown here says "3½ Floppy," but these little disks aren't floppy at all. They're hard plastic. They go into the drive with the metal tab going in first and the writing on the tab facing up.

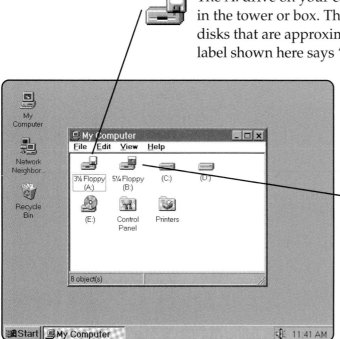

You may or may not have a B: drive like the computer shown in this example. The 5¼" disks are, in fact, floppy disks and bend easily. You insert these disks with the label held in your fingers and the print facing up.

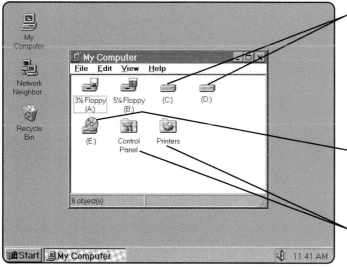

This computer has both a C: drive and a D: drive. Your computer may have only a C: drive. The C: and D: drives are the "hard drives" on your computer.

If you have a CD-ROM drive, you'll have an icon that looks like this one.

You can get to the Control Panel and the Printers dialog boxes by clicking twice on these icons.

LOOKING AT C: DRIVE

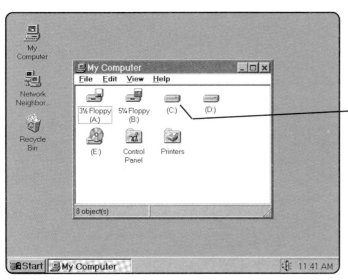

In this section, you'll look at the contents of your C: drive, which is the hard drive on your computer.

1. **Click twice** on the (C:) **drive icon**. The (C:) window will appear. The person who set up your computer may have labeled the drives differently from what you see here. The C: drive may have your name, for example, as part of the label.

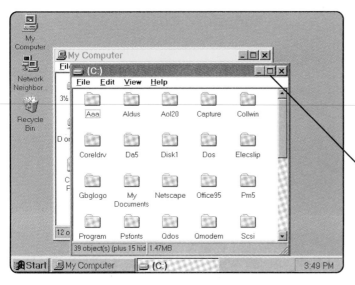

The (C:) window shows all the folders on your C: drive. You'll have different folders on your computer than are shown here. A folder was called a directory in Windows 3.1.

2. **Click** on the **Maximize button** (□) on the right side of the (C:) title bar to make the window fill your screen.

CHANGING THE VIEW

Your window may not look like the one in this example. It's easy to change the view, however.

Showing Small Icons

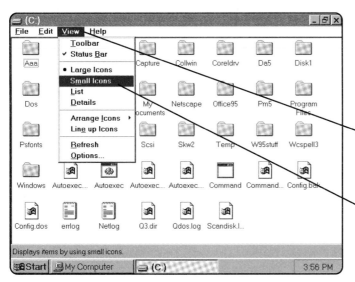

The information in the (C:) window doesn't change when you change the view. Only the presentation format changes.

1. **Click** on **View** in the menu bar. The View menu will appear.

2. **Click** on **Small Icons**. The view will change to the one shown below.

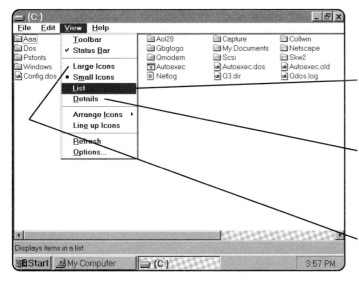

Showing Other Views

1. **Repeat steps 1 and 2** above, but **click** on **List** to see what the List view looks like.

2. **Repeat steps 1 and 2** above, but **click** on **Details** to see what the Details view looks like.

3. **Repeat steps 1 and 2** to go back to the **Large Icons**.

MAKING A NEW FOLDER

Folders help organize your computer just like folders in a file cabinet keep related information in one place. You can create a new folder at any time. In this section, you'll create a folder for memos.

1. Click on **File** in the menu bar. The File menu will appear.

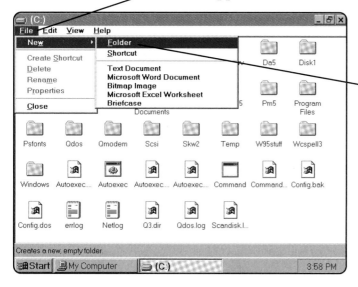

2. Move the pointer to **New**. A second menu will appear.

3. Click on **Folder**. A new folder will be placed at the end of the icons in this window.

Naming a New Folder

The name "New Folder" is already highlighted, so you can just begin typing.

1. Type Memos as the name for the new folder. Memos will replace the highlighted text.

The next time you save a memo, you can put it in the Memos folder instead of in the My Documents folder. (See pages 131 to 132 in Chapter 12 for directions on "Naming and Saving the Memo.")

ARRANGING FOLDERS

In this example, you'll arrange the folders alphabetically by name.

1. Click on **View** in the menu bar. The View menu will appear.

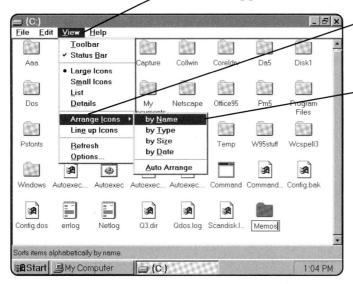

2. Move the mouse pointer to **Arrange Icons**. A second menu will appear.

3. Click on **by Name**. The folders will be rearranged alphabetically by name.

4. Click anywhere to remove the highlighting from the folder.

ADDING A TOOLBAR

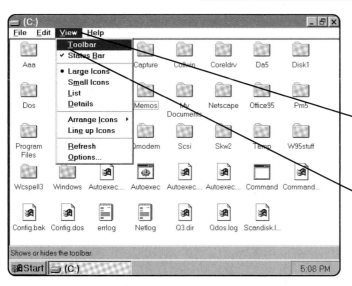

You can add a toolbar that contains icons for common operations, such as copy, cut, and paste.

1. Click on **View** in the menu bar. The View menu will appear.

2. Click on **Toolbar**. A toolbar will be added to your screen below the menu bar.

USING DRAG-AND-DROP TO MOVE A FILE

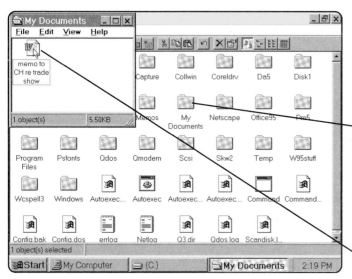

In this example, you'll move the "memo to CH" that is in the My Documents folder to the newly created Memos folder.

1. Click twice on the **My Documents folder** to open it, as you see here. You'll see an icon for the "memo to CH re trade show" that you created in Chapter 12.

2. Place the mouse arrow on **top** of the **file icon**.

3. Press and hold the mouse button and drag the icon to the **Memos folder**. You'll see a shadow icon move as you drag.

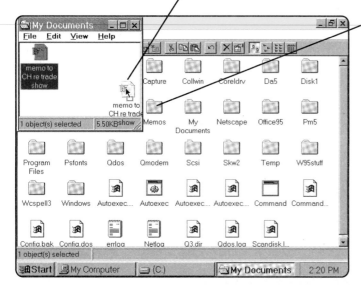

4. Place the **shadow icon** on **top** of the **Memos folder** and **release** the mouse button. The file will be put into the Memos folder. My Documents will close.

Note: If you hold the Shift key as you drag, the file will be copied rather than moved.

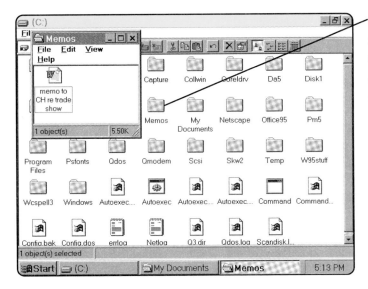

5. **Click twice** on the **Memos folder**. It will open, as you see here. Notice that the file for "memo to CH re trade show" is now in this folder.

MOVING A FILE WITH CUT-AND-PASTE

In this example, you'll cut the memo file from the Memos folder and paste it back into My Documents.

1. **Click** the *right* **mouse button** on **memo to CH re trade show**. A pop-up menu will appear.

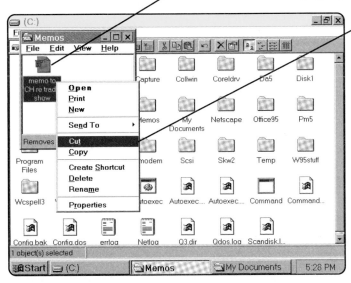

2. **Click** on **Cut**. The file will be cut from the folder. It will still appear in the folder, but if you look carefully, you'll see that the file icon is very faint. When the folder is closed, the file will disappear from the folder.

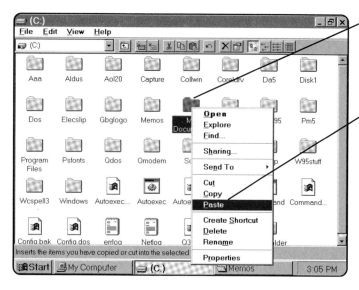

3. **Click** the *right* mouse button on the **My Documents folder**. A pop-up menu will appear.

4. **Click** on **Paste**. The file will be pasted into the My Documents folder. (You can open the folder and check if you want.)

DELETING A FOLDER

In this example, you'll delete the Memos folder by using the toolbar.

1. **Click** on the **Memos folder** to highlight it.

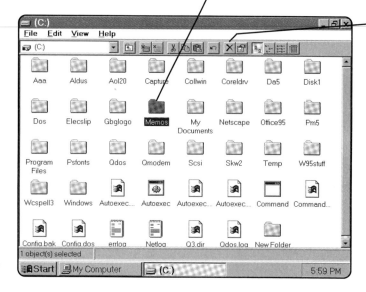

2. **Click** on the **X** in the toolbar. A Confirm Folder Delete dialog box will appear.

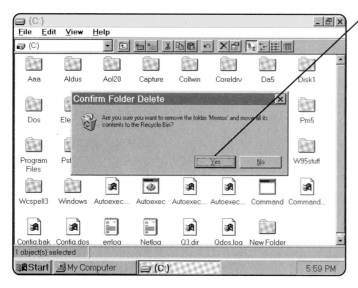

3. **Click** on **Yes** to delete the folder. When you delete a folder, all its contents are sent to the Recycle Bin. You'll learn how to use the Recycle Bin in Chapter 18. Even when a folder is empty, as is the case with the Memos folder, you'll get this message.

When the folder is deleted, it leaves a hole in the list of icons.

4. **Repeat steps 1 through 3** in "Arranging Folders" on page 173 to rearrange the icons and fill in the hole.

The same procedures that you use in My Computer to manage your files can be used in Explorer. You'll learn about Explorer in the next chapter. In Explorer, you'll learn some additional procedures beyond those you learned in this chapter.

5. **Click** on the **Close button** ([X]) to close the (C:) window.

CHECKING YOUR DISK SPACE

Disk space is like closet space: The more you have, the more programs and files you can have on your computer. There is another side to the coin, however. The more space you have, the more junk you tend to accumulate. It's a good idea to check your free disk space occasionally and then clean out unused programs and back up old files to a disk or tape drive (see Chapter 20). Before you install a new program, it's a good idea to check to make sure that you have enough room on your hard drive. Today's programs tend to require lots of space.

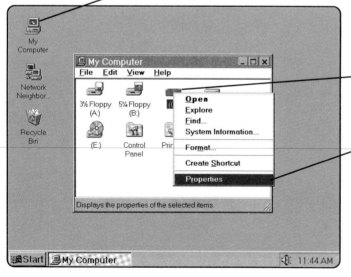

1. Click twice on **My Computer** to open the My Computer window you see here. If you've been following along with this chapter, it is already on your screen.

2. Click the *right* **mouse button** on the (C:) drive icon. A pop-up menu will appear.

3. Click on **Properties**. The (C:) Properties dialog box will appear.

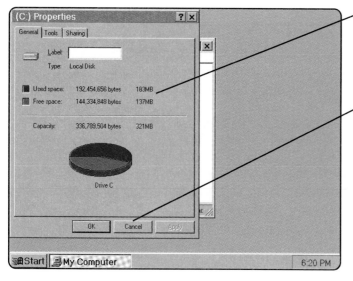

Notice the amount of used and free space as well as the total space available on this drive.

4. Click on **Cancel** to close the (C:) Properties window.

5. Click on the **Close button** ([X]) on the right side of the My Computer window to close it.

FINDING A FILE

Sometimes a file gets saved to the wrong folder, or you simply forget where you put the silly thing. Use the Start menu to search for a file.

1. Click on the **Start button** on the Taskbar. A pop-up menu will appear.

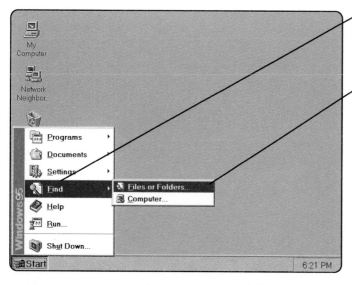

2. Move the mouse arrow to **Find**. Another menu will appear.

3. Click on **Files or Folders**. The Find All Files dialog box will appear.

In this example, you'll search for "memo to CH re trade show" that you created in Chapter 12. However, let's pretend that you don't remember the exact name of the file and that all you can remember is that it was "memo"-something-or-other.

4. **Click** on the **Name & Location tab** if it is not already in the front.

5. **Type memo*.*** in the Named box. The *.* (star period star) tells Windows to search for all files that start with "memo" no matter what the rest of the name may be. The *.* is called a *wildcard*.

Notice that (C:) is already in the Look in box. This means that Windows will look for the file on the C: drive. If you want to look in another drive, click on the ▼ to the right of the box, and then click on the drive you want to search.

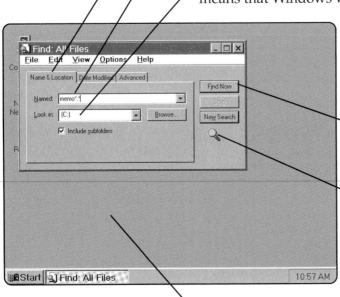

6. **Click** on **Find Now**. Windows will begin to search.

Notice the moving magnifying glass as the search progresses. Clever people, these Windows programmers!

When the search is complete, you'll see the list of possible matches in the bottom section of the dialog box.

7. **Click** on the **Maximize button** (□) on the right of the title bar to increase the size of the window.

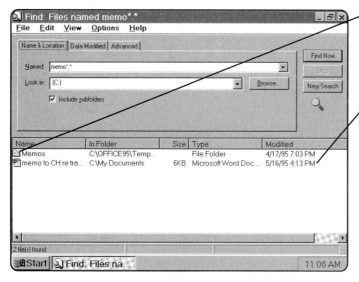

Notice that the first item on this list is a folder called "Memos" located on C: drive in the Office 95 folder.

The file we're looking for is the second item on the list. It is located on C: drive in My Documents. The listing also gives you the size of the file, the type, and the date and time it was created or modified. Notice that "memo to CH re trade show" is listed as a Microsoft Word Document. This is because WordPad saves documents as Word documents. If you click twice on this listing, it will open the document in Word. We won't show that here.

CLEARING A FILE SEARCH

If you want to search for a different file, you have to clear the file list at the bottom of the window.

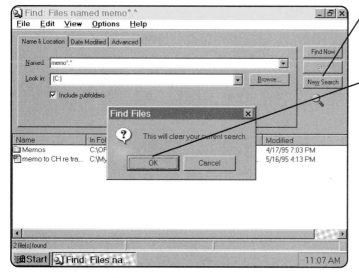

1. **Click** on **New Search**. The Find Files question box you see here will appear.

2. **Click** on **OK**. The list of files will be cleared from the window.

3. **Click** on the **Close button** ([×]) on the right side of the Find Files title bar when you've completed your searches.

Managing Files with Explorer

All the tasks you can do in My Computer, you can do in Explorer. If you're used to Windows 3.1, check out Explorer. Explorer is the new and improved version of File Manager. In this chapter, you will do the following:

✔ Create and name a new folder

✔ Move and delete files

✔ Copy a file from your computer to a disk in A: drive

✔ Move a file from a disk in A: drive to a folder on C: drive

OPENING EXPLORER

In this example, you'll use the Start menu to open Explorer.

1. Click on the **Start button** on the taskbar. A pop-up menu will appear.

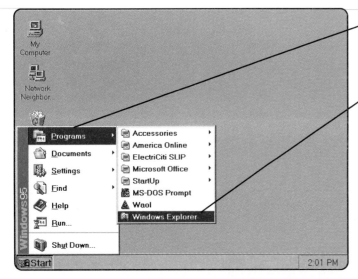

2. Move the mouse arrow to **Programs**. Another menu will appear.

3. Click on **Windows Explorer**. The Exploring - (C:) window will appear.

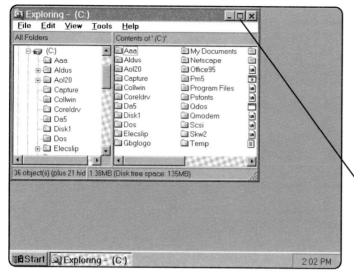

CHANGING THE VIEW

Your Explorer window may appear in a different spot and in a different size from the window in this example.

1. **Click** on the **Maximize button** (☐) on the right side of the Explorer title bar to make the window fill the screen.

Adding a Toolbar

If your window does not look like this one, the view is easily changed. In this example, you'll add the toolbar so that you can change the view with a click of your mouse.

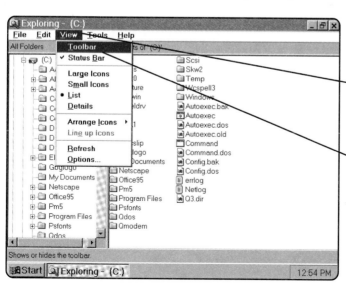

1. **Click** on **View** in the toolbar. The View menu will appear.

2. **Click** on **Toolbar**. A toolbar will be added below the menu bar.

Showing a List of Folders and Files

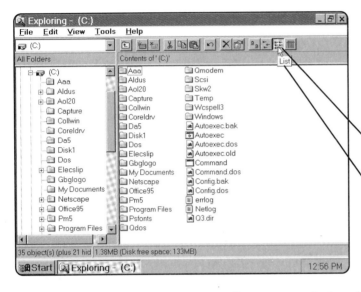

One of the available views in Explorer is the list view, which is shown here. If you want your screen to look like the examples in this chapter, do the following:

1. **Click** on the **List button** on the toolbar.

Notice that an identifying label appears when you rest the mouse arrow on top of the button.

2. **Point** your **mouse arrow** at the other buttons on your toolbar to see what each one does.

SEEING WHAT'S ON YOUR COMPUTER

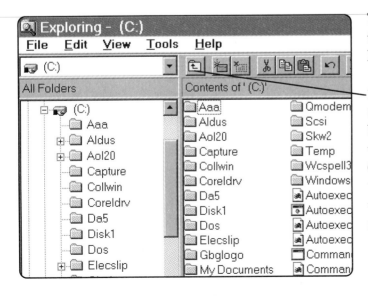

The folders on the left side of the window are arranged in levels.

1. **Click** on the **folder button** (called the Up One Level button) on the toolbar. This will take you up to My Computer, which is one "level" above (C:). You'll see what that means in the following examples.

EXPANDING AND CONTRACTING FOLDERS

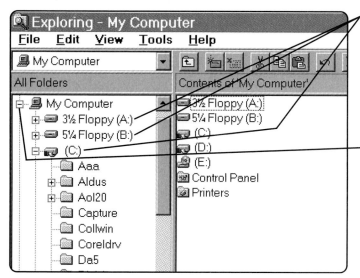

Notice that (A:) drive, (B:) drive, and (C:) drive are indented under My Computer because these drives are all part of My Computer.

1. **Click** on the ⊟ **icon** to the left of My Computer. All levels below My Computer will be closed and put into the My Computer level.

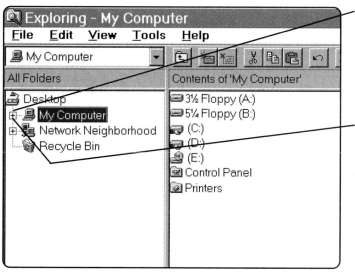

Notice that My Computer now has a ⊞ icon beside it, which shows that this level has sublevels and can be expanded.

2. **Click** on the ⊞ **icon** beside My Computer to open this level and show all the folders below it.

SEEING THE CONTENTS OF A FOLDER

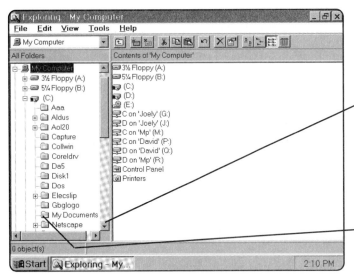

In this section, you'll look at the My Documents folder. If you don't have this folder, look at another one.

1. Click on the ▼ on the scroll bar until you can see My Documents on the left side of the window. You may be able to see My Documents without scrolling.

2. Click on **My Documents** (or another folder if you don't have My Documents).

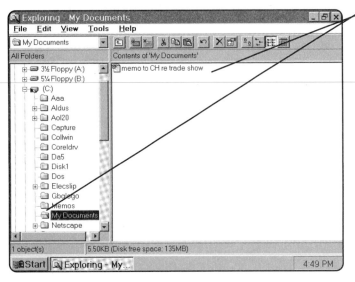

Notice that the folder "opens" and the documents in the folder appear on the right side of the window. If you've been following along with the chapters in this book, there is a file called "memo to CH re trade show" that was created in Chapter 12. Otherwise, this folder may be empty.

CREATING AND NAMING A NEW FOLDER

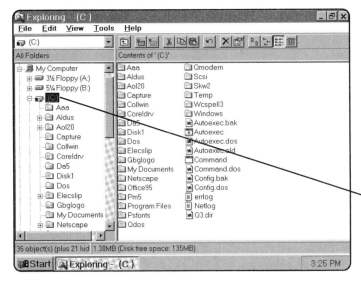

Most of the folders on your computer were put there by Windows or other programs when they were installed. You can create folders for your own files. In this section, you'll create a folder called "Memos" that you can use to hold memos you write.

1. Click on **(C:)** to tell your computer that you want to create a folder on the C: drive.

2. Click on **File** in the menu bar. The File menu will appear.

3. Click on **New**. A second menu will appear.

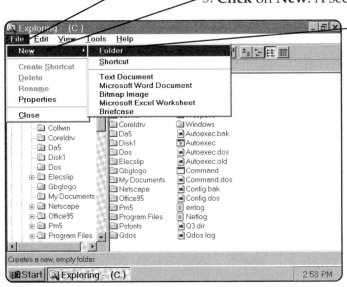

4. Click on **Folder**. A new folder will be added to the end of the list on the right side of the window.

Note: If you forget to click on (C:) (step 1) and you do steps 2 through 4 while a folder such as My Documents is highlighted, you will create a subfolder of My Documents. That's okay if that is what you want to do.

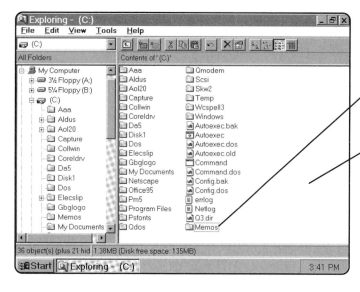

Notice on your screen that New Folder is highlighted in the box next to the folder.

5. Type Memos. It will replace the highlighted text.

6. Click in the **clear space** on the screen to remove the box around Memos.

SORTING FOLDERS

In this example, you'll sort the folders alphabetically.

1. Click on **View** in the menu bar. The View menu will appear.

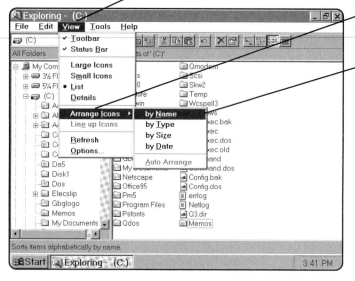

2. Click on **Arrange Icons**. Another menu will appear.

3. Click on **by Name**. The folders and files in the list will be arranged alphabetically by name.

Notice the items at the end of the list. These are technical files that have to do with the operation of the computer or a specific program. You will see different files on your screen.

MOVING A FILE TO ANOTHER FOLDER

In this section, you'll move a file from the My Documents folder into the Memos folder.

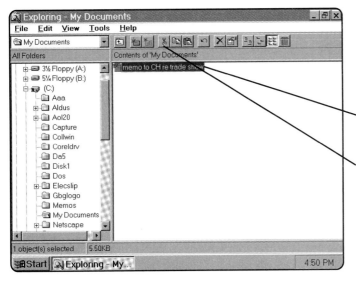

1. Click on **My Documents** to open the folder. The files in the folder will appear on the right side of the window.

2. Click on **memo to CH re trade show** to highlight it.

3. Click on the **Cut button** in the toolbar. The file will be cut from the folder. You'll still be able to see the file, but it will be very faint. It will disappear completely when you go to another folder.

4. Click on the **Memos** folder to highlight it.

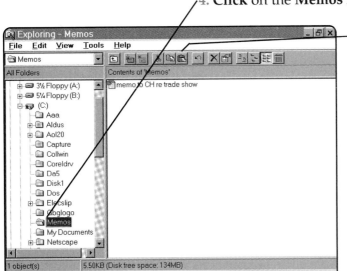

5. Click on the **Paste button** in the toolbar. The memo will be pasted into the Memos folder, as you see here.

UNDOING A MOVE

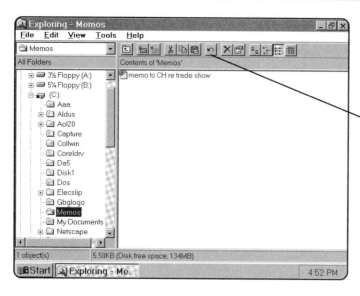

If you decide that you don't want to move the file you moved in the last example, you can use the Undo button.

1. Click on the **Undo button** in the toolbar. The file will be taken out of the Memos folder and put back into the My Documents folder. (Why don't you open the My Documents folder and check?)

DELETING A FOLDER

In this section, you'll delete the Memos folder.

1. Click on the **Memos folder** to highlight it.

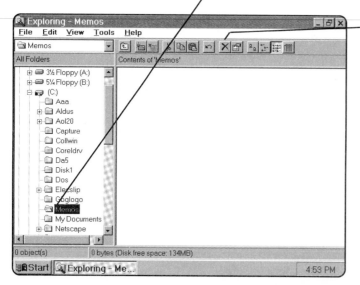

2. Click on the **Delete button** in the toolbar. The Confirm Folder Delete dialog box will appear.

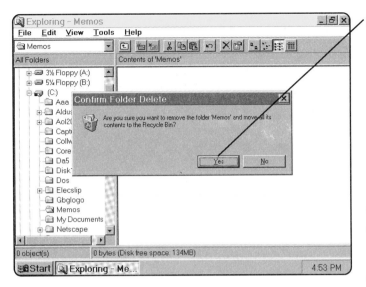

3. **Click** on **Yes**.

COPYING A FILE TO A DISK IN A: DRIVE

If you've been working on a file at home and want to bring it into work, copy the file to a disk. In this section, you'll copy the memo to CH to a disk.

1. **Insert** a **disk** into A: drive.

2. **Click** on **My Documents** to open the folder.

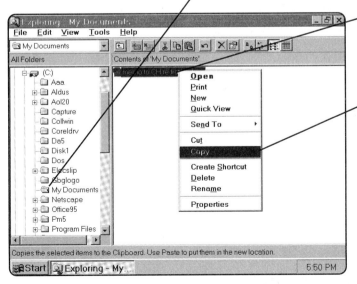

3. **Click** the *right* **mouse button** on **memo to CH re trade show**. A pop-up menu will appear.

4. **Click** on **Copy**. You won't see any difference in your screen, but the file has been copied to the *Clipboard*, a temporary storage area on your computer.

Note: You can use the pop-up menus or the button on the toolbar to do the same tasks.

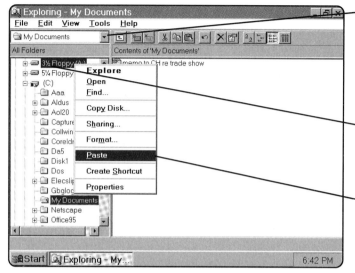

5. **Click** on the ▲ on the scroll bar to scroll up the list of folders until you see the (A:) drive. (You may not have to scroll on your computer.)

6. **Click** the *right* **mouse button** on the **(A:) drive icon**. A pop-up menu will appear.

7. **Click** on **Paste**. You'll see a really cute, moving graphic of a file being copied from one folder to another.

MOVING A FILE FROM A DISK TO YOUR HARD DRIVE

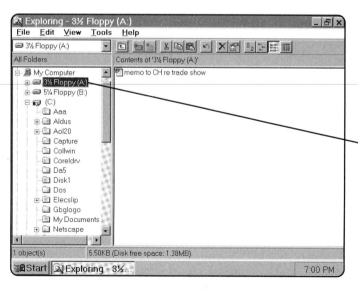

In this section, you'll move a file from a disk in A: drive to the My Documents folder.

1. **Insert** the appropriate **disk** into A: drive.

2. **Click** on the **(A:) drive icon** on the left side of your screen. Notice that (A:) now shows in the drive box. (You can also select a drive by clicking on the ▲ to the right of the drive box and clicking on (A:) drive.)

3. **Click** on the **file** you want to move to highlight it.

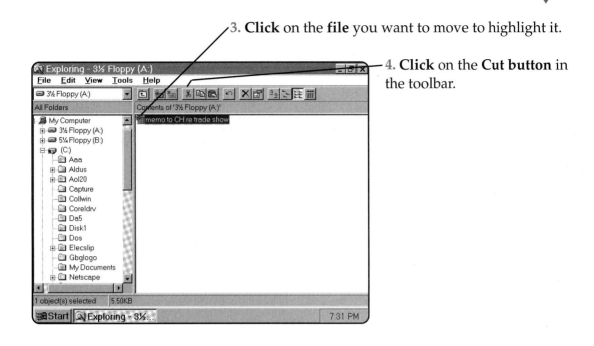

4. **Click** on the **Cut button** in the toolbar.

5. **Click** on the **My Documents** folder to open it.

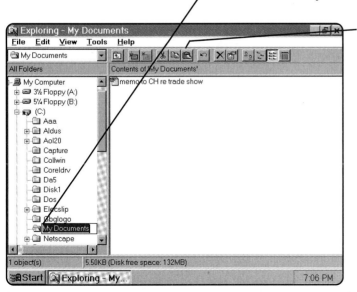

6. **Click** on the **Paste button** in the toolbar. After a pause, you'll see the Confirm File Replace dialog box.

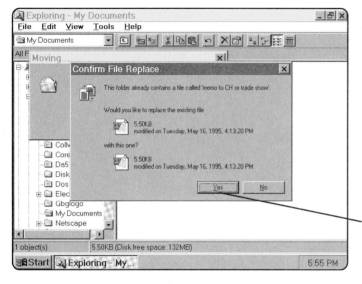

You're seeing this dialog box because Windows knows that "memo to CH re trade show" is already in the My Documents folder. It is asking if you want to replace the version that is currently in the folder with the version you are moving from A: Drive.

7. **Click** on **Yes** to replace the file currently in the folder.

USING QUICK VIEW

Sometimes you forget what a file is all about. You can get a quick preview in Explorer.

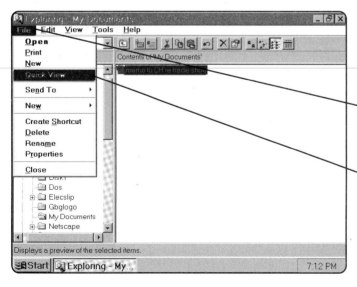

1. **Click** on **memo to CH re trade show** in the My Documents folder to highlight it.

2. **Click** on **File** in the menu bar. The File menu will appear.

3. **Click** on **Quick View**. After a pause, a window will appear, showing the file. If Quick View is not on this menu, see the Note at the end of the next page.

You can open this file for editing by clicking on the first icon in the toolbar. We won't show that here.

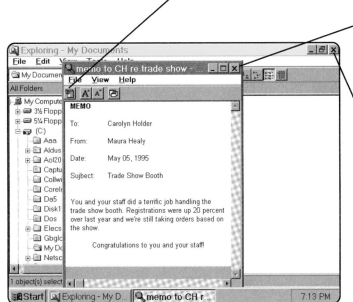

4. Click on the Close button ([x]) on the title bar to close the Quick View window.

5. Click on the Close button on the Explorer title bar to close Explorer.

Note: If Quick View is not on the File menu, there are two possible reasons:

❖ No file viewer is available for the type of file you have highlighted.

❖ Quick View is not installed on your computer. You can install it very easily. See the first few pages in Chapter 20, "Backing Up Files and Folders" and follow the process described in "Installing the Backup Program" to install Quick View.

Using and Clearing the Recycle Bin

When you delete a file, a folder, an icon, or a shortcut in Windows 95, it goes to the Recycle Bin where it is held until the Recycle Bin is cleared. This means that you cannot delete a file by accident. You can check the contents of the Recycle Bin and restore a file if you don't want it to be deleted. The cost of having this ability, however, is that the files in the Recycle Bin take up space on your hard drive. Clear the Recycle Bin on a regular basis to make sure that you have as much work space on your hard drive as possible. In this chapter, you will do the following:

✔ Delete a file

✔ Restore a file that has been sent to the Recycle Bin

✔ Clear the Recycle Bin

GETTING READY FOR THIS CHAPTER

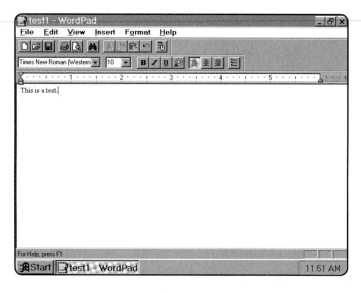

In the first part of this chapter, you'll learn how to delete a file from a folder. If you want to follow along with the steps, we suggest that you create two "test" files to delete.

1. **Open WordPad** and **type** the **text** you see here.

2. **Save** the **file** with the name "test1" in the My Documents folder. See Chapter 12 if you need help.

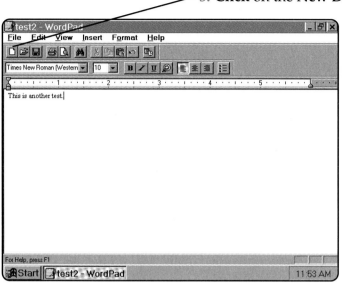

3. Click on the **New Document icon**. It's the first icon in the toolbar. A new document screen will appear.

4. Create a **second file** like the one you see here, and name it "test2."

5. Close WordPad.

Now you have three files in the My Documents folder.

SENDING A FILE TO THE RECYCLE BIN

You can delete a file by using My Computer or Explorer. The examples in this section will use My Computer.

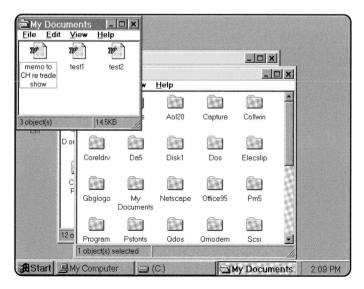

1. Open the **My Documents folder** on your C drive. See Chapter 16 if you need help.

Notice that this view in My Documents shows large icons. If your view is different and you want it to look like these examples, see Chapter 16 for help in switching to the large icon view.

In this example, My Documents shows three files: the "memo to CH re trade show" that was created in Chapter 12 and the two test files.

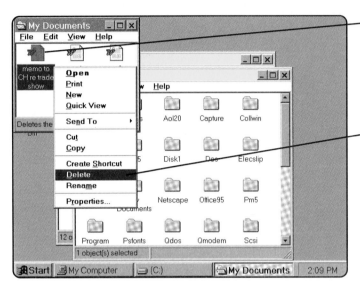

2. Click the *right* **mouse button** on the **file** you want to delete. In this example, it is "memo to CH re trade show." A pop-up menu will appear.

3. Click on **Delete**. The Confirm File Delete dialog box will appear.

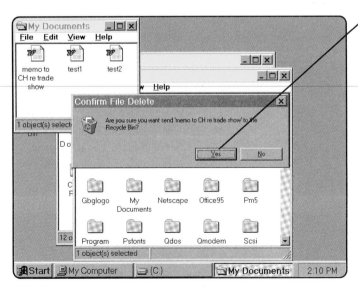

4. Click on **Yes** to tell Windows that "Yes, I'm sure I want to delete this file."

Notice that the memo to CH has been deleted from the folder.

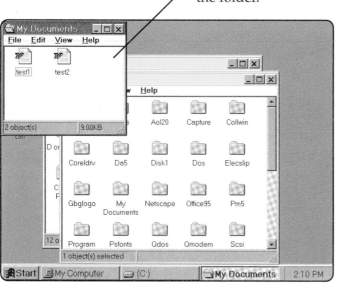

UNDOING A DELETION WITH THE EDIT MENU

There is more than one way to do most everything in Windows. If you recognize immediately that you deleted a file in error, you can use the Edit menu to get it back.

1. Click on **Edit** in the menu bar. The Edit menu will appear.

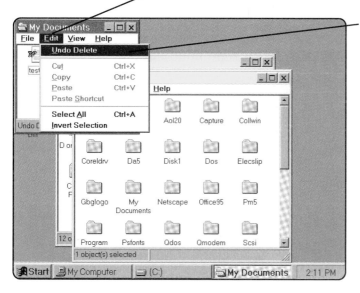

2. Click on **Undo Delete**. The deleted file will be restored to the folder.

3. Click on the **Close button** (⊠) to close the My Documents folder.

DELETING MORE THAN ONE FILE AT A TIME

You can delete multiple files at the same time. In this section, you'll delete the two test files.

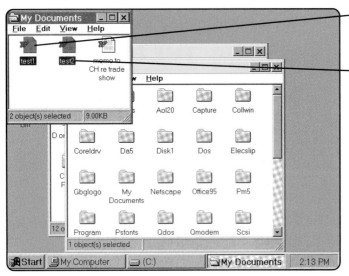

1. Click on **test1** to highlight it.

2. Press and hold the **Shift key** and **click** on **test2**. Both files will be highlighted. (Normally, you can highlight only one file at a time. Holding the Shift key allows you to select consecutive files.)

3. Place the mouse arrow on one of the highlighted files and **press** the *right* **mouse button**. A pop-up menu will appear.

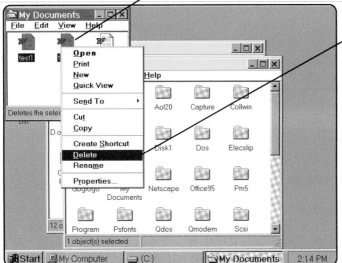

4. Click on **Delete**. A Confirm File Delete dialog box (not shown here) will ask if you're sure that you want to send the files to the Recycle Bin.

5. Click on **Yes**.

RESTORING A FILE FROM THE RECYCLE BIN

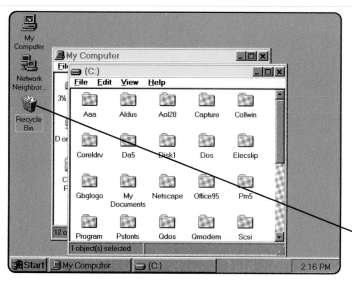

It's easy to restore a file that has been sent to the Recycle Bin. You can get to the Recycle Bin by several routes. In this section, you'll use the Recycle Bin icon that is on your desktop.

You can open the Recycle Bin at any time regardless of what's on your screen.

1. Click twice on the **Recycle Bin icon**. The Recycle Bin window will appear.

If you have lots of data in the Recycle Bin, you can click on the Maximize button (□) to enlarge the window. In this example, you'll leave the window in the size in which it appears.

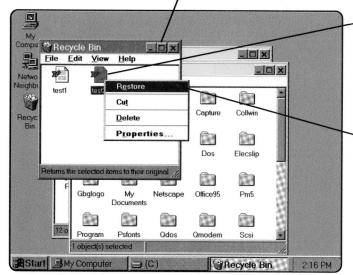

2. Click the *right* **mouse button** on the **file** you want to restore. In this example, it is test2. A pop-up menu will appear.

3. Click on **Restore**. The file will be returned to its original folder.

EMPTYING THE RECYCLE BIN

Shutting down your computer will not empty the Recycle Bin. You must manually go into the Recycle Bin and empty it. Deleted files that are sent to the Recycle Bin stay there and take up space on your hard drive. Therefore, it's a good idea to empty the Recycle Bin on a regular basis to free up this space.

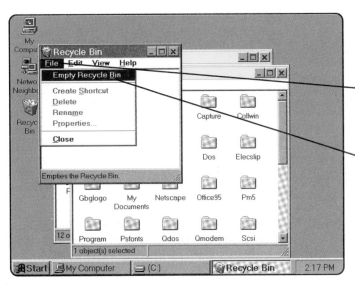

1. Click twice on the **Recycle Bin icon** on your desktop if you haven't already done so.

2. Click on **File** in the menu bar. The File menu will appear.

3. Click on **Empty Recycle Bin**. The Confirm File Delete dialog box will appear.

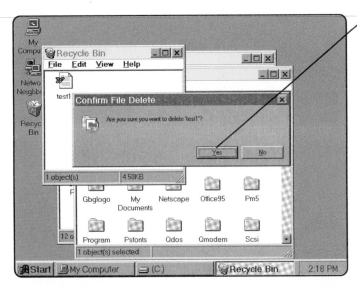

4. Click on **Yes** to empty the Recycle Bin.

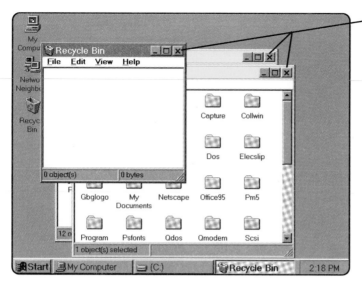

5. **Click** on the **Close buttons** ([X]) for the Recycle Bin, the C drive window, and the My Computer window to close them.

USING THE RECYCLE BIN THROUGH EXPLORER

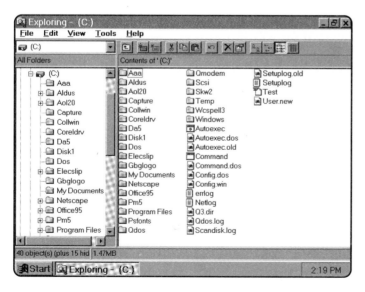

In this section, you'll go to Explorer and use the Recycle Bin.

1. **Open Explorer**. Refer to Chapter 17 if you need help.

Notice that the view in this example shows small icons and a toolbar. If your view in Explorer doesn't look like this and you want your screen to look like these examples, see Chapter 17.

2. **Click** on **My Documents** on the left side of the Explorer window. The folder will open, and the files in the folder will appear on the right side of the window.

Notice that the title bar reflects that My Documents is the open folder.

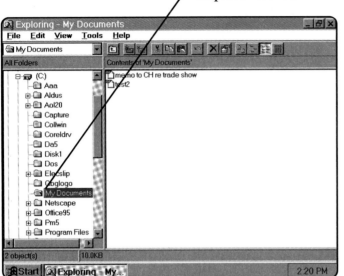

3. **Click** on the **first file** you want **to delete** to highlight it.

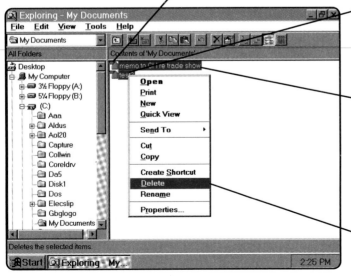

4. **Press and hold** the **Shift key** and **click** on the **second file**. Both files will be highlighted.

5. **Place** the mouse arrow on one of the highlighted files.

6. **Click** with the *right* **mouse button** on the **file** you want to delete. A pop-up menu will appear.

7. **Click** on **Delete**. The Confirm Multiple File Delete dialog box will appear.

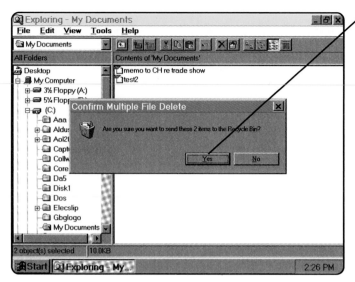

8. **Click** on **Yes** to delete the files. The files will be deleted from the My Documents folder and sent to the Recycle Bin.

USING THE RECYCLE BIN ON EXPLORER

When you're in Explorer, the Recycle Bin is listed on the left side of the window in the Folders list.

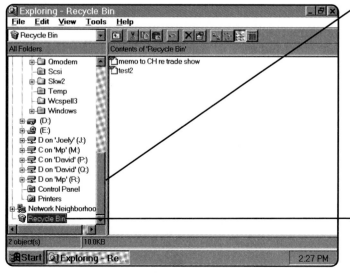

1. **Place** the mouse arrow on **top** of the **scroll button** on the scroll bar. It may be in a different spot on the scroll bar on your computer.

2. **Press and hold** the left mouse button as you **drag** the scroll button to the **bottom** of the scroll bar, as you see in this example.

3. **Click** on **Recycle Bin** to highlight it. A list of files in the Recycle Bin will show on the right.

Restoring a File in Explorer

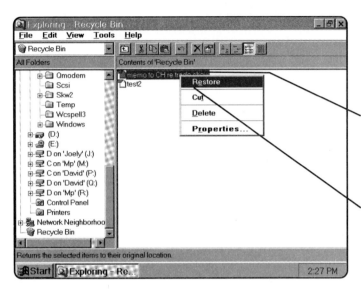

The process of restoring a file in Explorer is pretty much the same as it is when you use the Recycle Bin icon.

1. Click with the *right* mouse button on the file you want to restore. A pop-up menu will appear.

2. Click on Restore. The file will be sent back to its original folder.

Emptying the Recycle Bin in Explorer

1. Click with the *right* mouse button on Recycle Bin on the left side of the Explorer window. It will be highlighted, and a pop-up menu will appear.

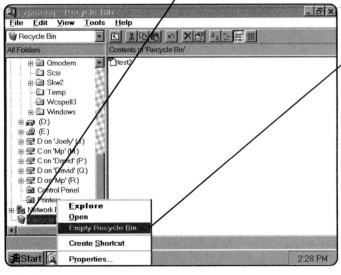

2. Click on Empty Recycle Bin. You'll see a Confirm File Delete dialog box (not shown here.)

3. Click on Yes.

4. Click on the Close button ([X]) to the right of the Explorer title bar to close it.

WINDOWS 95

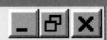

Part V: Managing Your Computer

Installing Software in Windows 95

Windows 95 has simplified the way you install programs. In fact, if your computer has a CD-Rom drive, the process is not only simple, it is very fast. In this chapter, you will do the following:

✔ Install Word 7 for Windows 95 as part of the Microsoft Office Installation.

INSERTING THE CD-ROM DISK

For some drives you may be required to place the CD-ROM disk into a special carrier before you insert the disk into the drive.

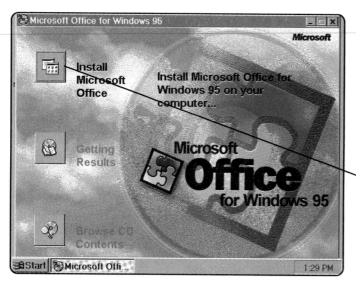

1. **Insert** your **CD-ROM** disk into your CD-ROM drive.

*If after a few minutes you **don't*** see the screen in this example, go directly to step 1 on page 259.

2. **Click** on **Install Microsoft Office**. The Microsoft Office for Windows '95 Setup dialog box will appear. Continue directly to step 4 on page 261.

OPENING THE CONTROL PANEL

1. Click on the **Start button** in the taskbar. A pop-up menu will appear.

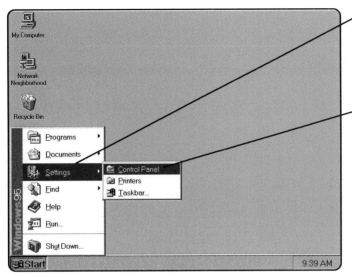

2. Move the **mouse arrow up** the menu to **Settings**. A second pop-up menu will appear.

3. Move the mouse arrow over to highlight **Control Panel**.

4. Click on **Control Panel**. The Control Panel dialog box will appear.

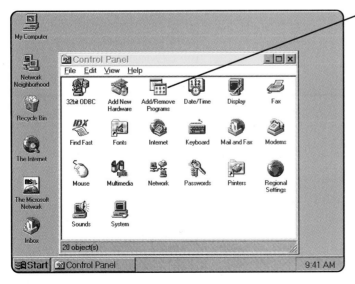

5. Click twice on **Add/Remove Programs**. The Add/Remove Program Properties dialog box will appear.

INSTALLING A PROGRAM

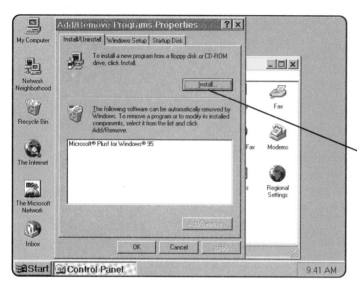

The following sections illustrate an installation using a CD-ROM disk. If you're using floppy disks for your installation, your screens will vary from these examples.

1. Click on the **Install button**. The Install Program From Floppy Disk or CD-ROM dialog box will appear.

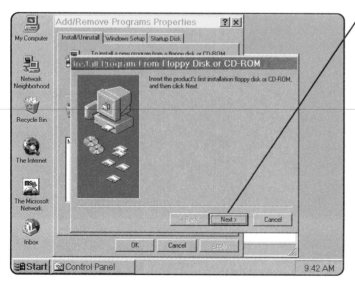

2. Click on **Next**. Windows 95 will quickly read drive A and drive B as it searches for the installation program. Once Windows 95 finds the installation program disk in the CD-ROM drive, the Run Installation Program message box will appear.

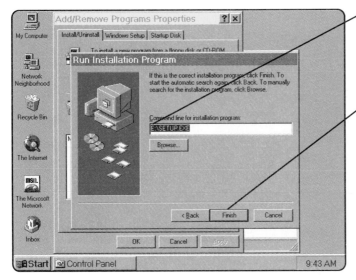

Notice that the command line for the installation automatically appears in the text box.

3. **Click** on **Finish**. The Setup Message box will appear.

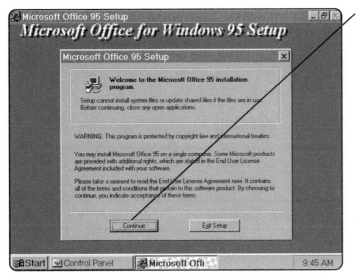

4. **Click** on **Continue**. The Name and Organization Information dialog box will appear.

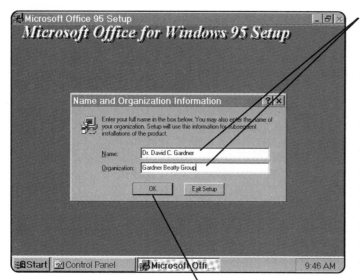

Notice that the name and organization information used in registering Windows 95 automatically appears in the text box below.

If this information is not correct, you can make the changes now. Or, you can fill in new information. Notice the cursor is flashing in the name text box. When you start typing, the cursor will disappear.

5. Click on **OK**. The Confirm Name and Organization Information dialog box will appear.

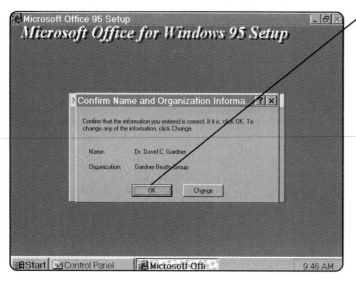

6. Click on **OK** if the information is correct. The Microsoft Office for Windows '95 Setup dialog box will appear.

If the information is not correct, **click** on **Change**. The previous dialog box will appear. After making your corrections, **click** on **OK** to return to this dialog box.

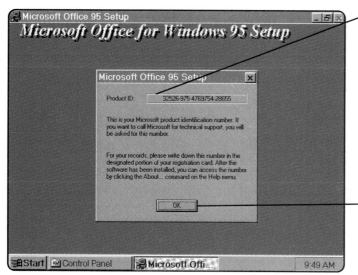

Notice that your product ID number appears on this screen. It is important that you make a note of the number and keep it handy. If you call Microsoft for technical support, you will need this number for identification.

8. **Click** on **OK**.

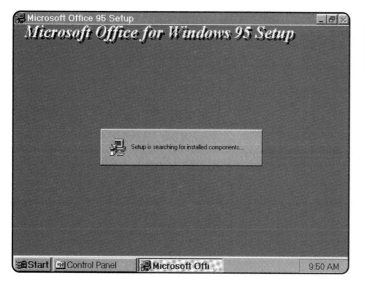

The hourglass will appear briefly along with a Microsoft message box that says "Setup is searching for installed components."

Selecting a Folder for MSOFFICE

Microsoft Office will automatically be installed to a new folder (directory) MSOFFICE which will be created on the C drive (C:\MSOFFICE).

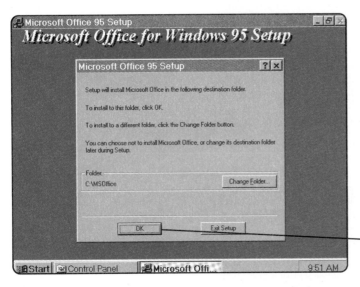

If, however, you wish to install this program in another directory (folder) or on another drive, click on the **Change Folder button**. A Change Directory dialog box will appear. **Type** in the new **folder (directory) name and path** and **click** on **OK**. A confirmation destination message box will appear. Click on Yes to confirm.

1. **Click** on **OK**. A Microsoft Office 95 Setup dialog box will appear.

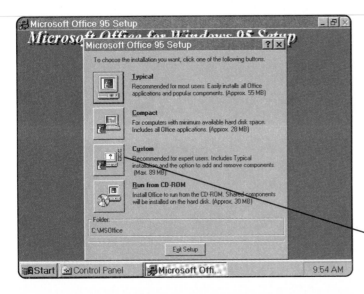

CUSTOMIZING AN INSTALL

You can, of course, click on Typical to install all the programs and the most used features. In this example, we'll show you some of what you can do in a customized installation.

1. **Click** on **Custom**. The Microsoft Office '95 Custom dialog box will appear.

Selecting Programs and Features

You can always add or remove programs and features at a later date by repeating the steps in this chapter.

1. Click in the **box** to *remove* the ✔ from any programs you *don't* want to install at this time.

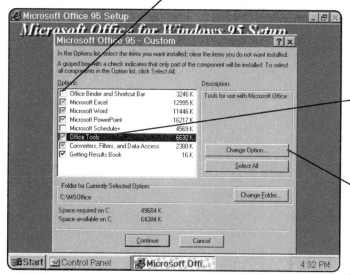

In this example, we won't install the Office Binder and Shortcut Bar or the Microsoft Schedule+.

2. Click on **the words "Office Tools" to highlight the line**. Don't click on the box or you'll remove the ✔.

3. Click on **Change Option**. The Microsoft Office 95 - Office Tools dialog box will appear.

Notice the "grayed-out" box to the left of Clip Art. This means that only some of the Clip Art options are to be installed. In this example, we'll change that to include all of the clip art.

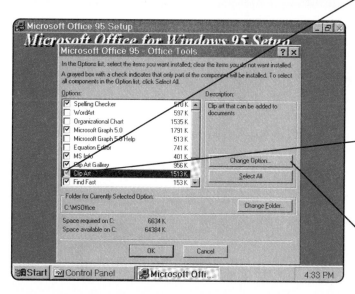

4. Click on the *words* **"Clip Art," to highlight the line**. Don't click on the box or you'll remove the ✔.

5. Click on **Change Options**. The Microsoft Office 95 - Clip Art dialog box will appear.

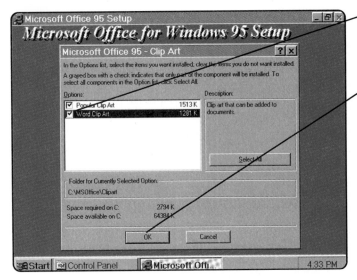

6. **Click** on **Word Clip Art** to place a ✔ in the box. The line will be highlighted.

7. **Click** on **OK**. The Clip Art dialog box will close.

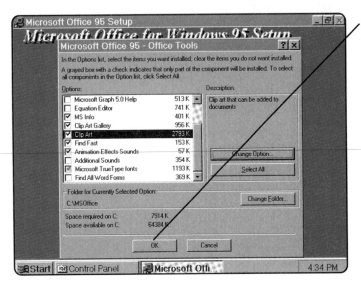

8. **Click** on **OK**. The Office Tools dialog box will close.

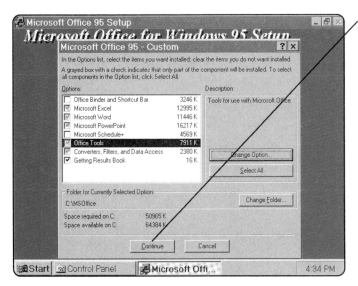

9. **Click** on **Continue**. The dialog box will close, and the Microsoft Office Setup: Disk 1 dialog box will appear.

Watching, Waiting

At this point sit back and relax. It's out of your hands. Using a CD-ROM certainly makes life easier. No more of the old "insert Disk #x routine."

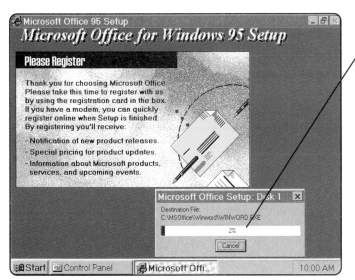

The Microsoft Office Setup: Disk 1 dialog box will show you the percentage of completion in copying files from the installation disk.

Soon the Setup dialog box will close and you'll see Microsoft Office for Windows 95 Restart dialog box.

Restarting Windows '95

At this point, you can register online.

1. If you want to register online, **click** on **Online Registration** and follow the directions on your screen.

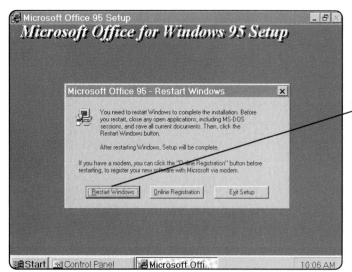

If you don't want to register online, you can send your registration information by mail.

2. Click on **Restart Windows**. You'll see the "Please wait while your computer shuts down" screen. Next, Windows 95 will automatically reopen and you'll see the Control Panel window on your screen.

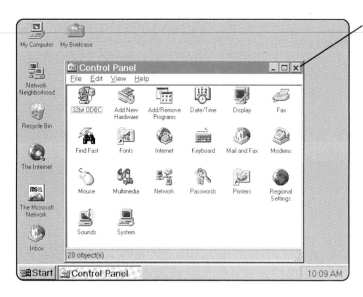

3. Click on the **close box** (⊠) to close the Control Panel.

VIEWING YOUR PROGRAMS

Now it's time to have fun and explore your new programs.

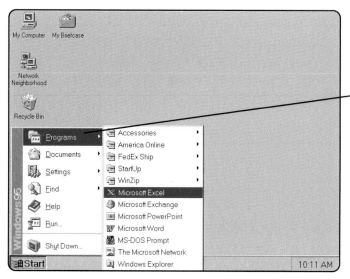

1. Click on the **Start button** on the taskbar. A pop-up menu will appear.

2. Move the **mouse arrow** up the menu to Programs. A second menu will appear.

Click on any of the programs . . . and you'll be on your way!

UNINSTALLING

✔ Uninstalling is just as easy as installing a program. We didn't illustrate it in this book, but the process couldn't be simpler. From the Add/Remove Programs dialog box (shown on page 210), simply click on the program you want to uninstall to highlight it and click on the Remove button.

✔ By the way, the Uninstall program requires that you insert the original program disk into the drive before it will uninstall. It seems very confusing to put the program disk into the drive when you want to uninstall, but that's the way it works.

Backing Up Files and Folders

As you may have noticed, Windows 95 comes fully equipped with all kinds of accessories. One accessory you may want to take advantage of is its backup program. You can back up your entire system to floppy disks, tapes, or optical disks and restore the files to your hard drive if the need arises with the Restore program. In this chapter, you will do the following:

✔ Install the Windows backup program

✔ Back up files to a floppy disk

✔ Restore the files to your hard drive

INSTALLING THE BACKUP PROGRAM

Windows comes with a great backup program. Depending on the way you installed Windows 95, you may not have it on your hard drive. In this example, you will install the backup program. If you already have it installed, go to the section entitled "Backing up to Floppy Disks" on page 225.

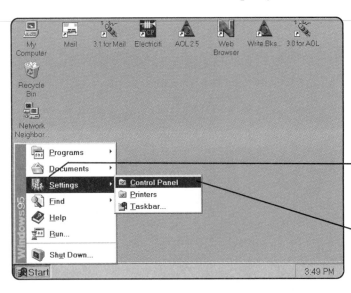

1. Click on **Start** in the left corner of the taskbar. A pop-up menu will appear.

2. Move the mouse arrow to **Settings**. Another menu will appear.

3. Click on **Control Panel**. The Control Panel window will appear.

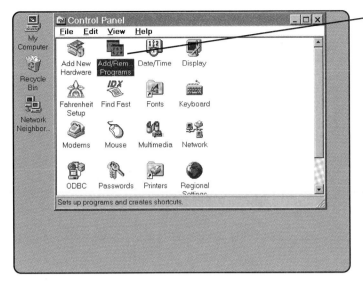

4. **Click twice** on the **Add/Remove Programs icon**. The Add/Remove Programs Properties dialog box will appear.

Note: If you inserted your Windows '95 CD-ROM disk before you started, you will get an hourglass intermission followed by a new screen showing a big CD-ROM picture. Simply click on the Add/Remove Programs icon in the lower right corner and go to step 6.

5. **Click** on the **Windows Setup tab** to bring it to the front.

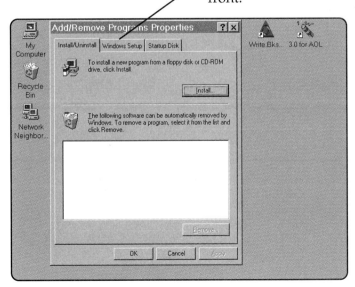

Note: If you need to remove a program that has been written specifically for Windows 95, this is the place to do it. Simply click on the Install/Uninstall tab if it is not already selected, and then click on the program you want to remove (not shown here). Next click on Remove and follow along. If you want to remove a program written for Windows 3.1 or DOS, you will need a special uninstall program, such as Uninstaller 2.0. Microsoft Office for 95 should be removed by using its own Setup program.

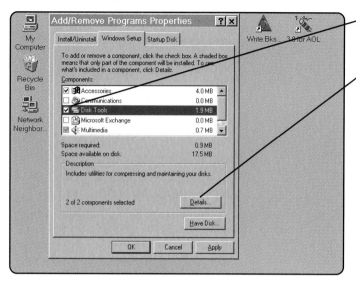

6. **Click** on **Disk Tools** to put a ✔ in the box.

7. **Click** on **Details**. The Disk Tools dialog box will appear.

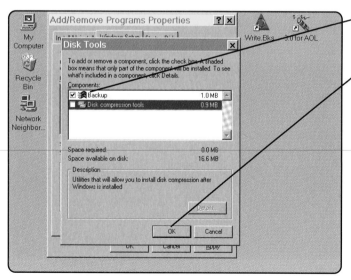

8. **Click** on **Backup** to put a ✔ in the box.

9. **Click** on **OK**. The dialog box will close.

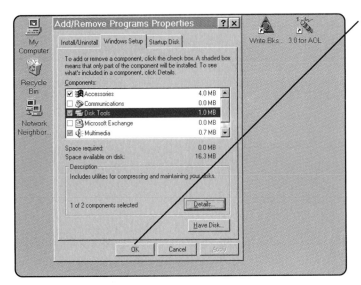

10. **Click** on **OK**. The Insert Disk dialog box will appear.

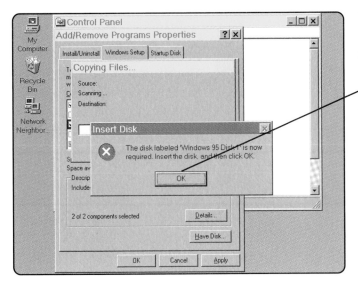

11. **Insert** your CD-ROM disk (or the disk number requested).

12. **Click** on **OK**. Windows will search for and find your Windows 95 CD-ROM or floppy disk. Next, the Copying Files dialog box will appear.

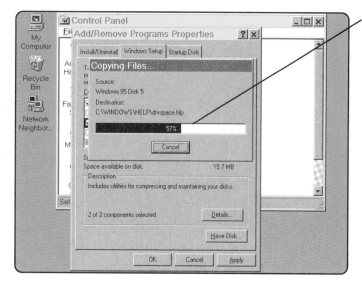

Notice that Windows keeps you informed of the copying progress.

When the copying is completed, a message box will appear briefly, letting you know that it is creating shortcuts for the new programs.

Next, the dialog box will close.

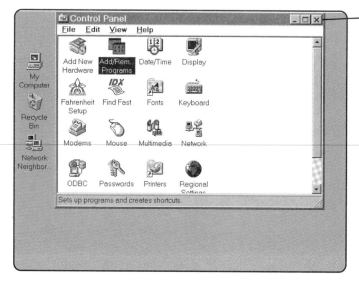

13. Click on the **Close button** ([X]) in the right corner of the title bar to close the window. The Windows 95 backup programs are now installed on your computer. You can back up to disks, tape, or an optical drive.

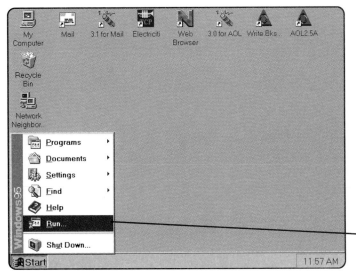

BACKING UP TO FLOPPY DISKS

In this section, you will back up selected files in a specific folder (directory) to a floppy disk.

1. Click on **Start**. A pop-up menu will appear.

2. Click on **Run**. The Run dialog box will appear.

Note: You can also start the backup program by clicking on a succession of menu choices, beginning with Start, and then going on to Programs, then Accessories, then System Tools, and, finally (at last), Backup.

3. Type backup.

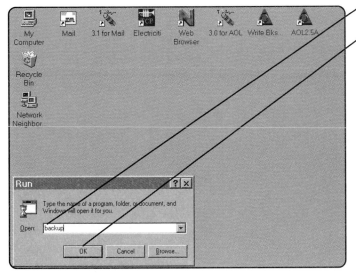

4. Click on **OK**. The Welcome to Microsoft Backup dialog box will appear.

Note: If you had a backup program installed prior to upgrading to Windows 95, this method for opening the backup program may not work because it may open the old program rather than the 95 backup program. In that case, follow the instructions in the Note above.

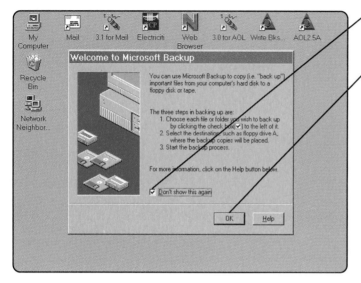

5. **Click** on **Don't show this again** to put a ✔ in the box.

6. **Click** on **OK**. The Microsoft Backup dialog box will appear.

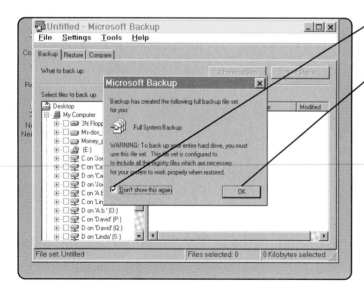

7. **Click** on **Don't show this again** to put a ✔ in the box.

8. **Click** on **OK**. The Untitled Microsoft Backup dialog box will appear.

Note: If you don't have a tape drive installed, you may get a dialog box about finding the tape drive. Just click on OK and the Backup dialog box will appear.

Selecting Files and Folders to Backup

With this flexible backup program, you can select entire folders or just files within folders to back up. In this example, you will select two files in the same folder to back up.

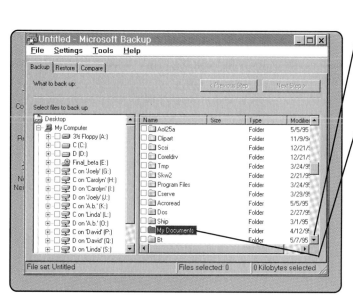

1. Click on the **hard drive** where the folder is located. A list of folders (directories) will appear in the right-hand box. In this example, we clicked on C (drive C:).

If you are not on a network, you won't see a list of drives, as shown here.

2. Click repeatedly on the ▼ to scroll down the list of folders until you find the folder you want.

3. Click twice on the **folder**. The list of files contained in the folder will be shown in the right-hand box. In this example, we clicked on the folder My Documents.

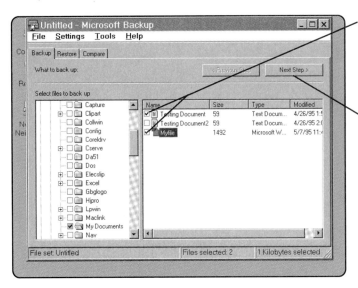

4. Click on the **files**, one after the other, that you want to back up to put a ✔ in the box.

5. Click on **Next Step**. The title "Select a destination for the backup" will appear in the left box.

6. Click on your **floppy drive/location** to highlight it. In this example, we clicked on 3½ Floppy (A:).

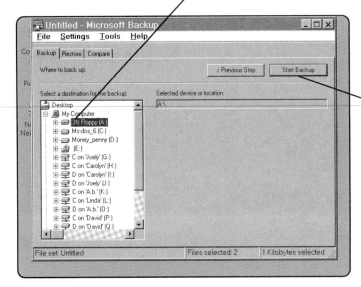

7. Insert a **disk** in the drive you selected. In this example, we chose drive A.

8. Click on **Start Backup**. The Backup Set Label dialog box will appear.

Naming the Backup File

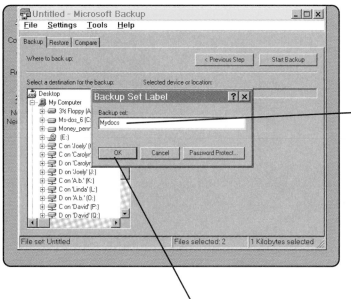

All the files and folders you selected to back up will be compressed into one file. Windows requires that you give it a name.

1. **Type** a **name** for the backup file.

Completing the Backup

Now that you have selected the files and named the backup file, backing up is easy!

1. **Click** on **OK**. The Backup dialog box will appear.

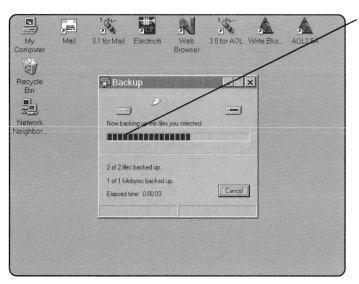

Notice that Windows keeps you informed of the backup process. When the process is complete, a message box will appear.

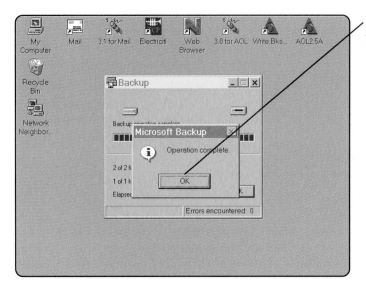

2. **Click** on **OK**. The dialog box will close.

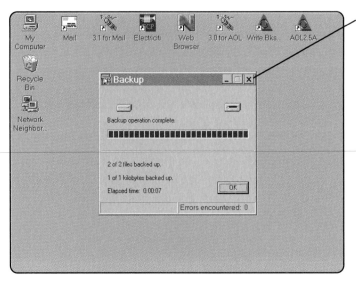

3. **Click** on the **Close button** ([×]) in the right corner of the title bar to close the dialog box. The Untitled Microsoft Backup dialog box will appear. You can close that dialog box by repeating this step. If you want to follow along to the next section, do not close it.

4. Remove the disk from drive A. The files are all backed up!

Note: As of this writing, the backup files you create in Windows 95 are not compatible with Windows 3.1 backup programs. To restore them to another computer, it must be running Windows 95's backup program.

RESTORING BACKED-UP FILES

We hope that you won't have to restore your files very often, but if you do, it couldn't be easier.

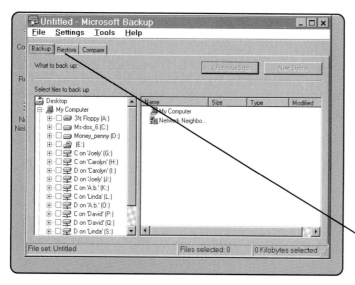

1. Repeat steps 1 through 8 in the section entitled "Backing Up to Floppy Disks" to open the dialog box shown here if you did not leave it open in the previous section.

2. Insert the **disk** containing your backup file(s) into your floppy drive (drive A).

3. Click on **Restore**. The Restore tab will move to the front.

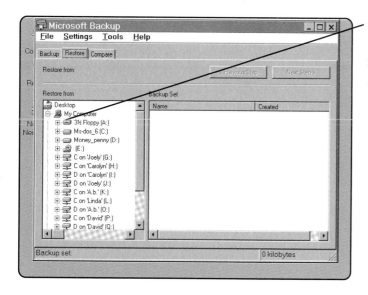

4. Click on **3½ floppy** (A:) in the Restore from box. The name of your backup file will appear in the right-hand box.

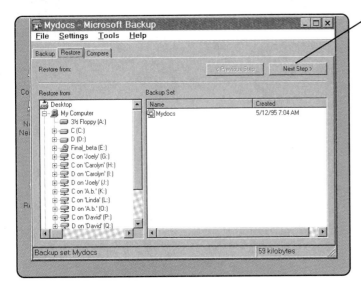

5. **Click** on **Next Step**. After an hourglass intermission, the name of your backup file (in this example, Mydocs) will appear in the box on the left, and "C:" will appear in the box on the right.

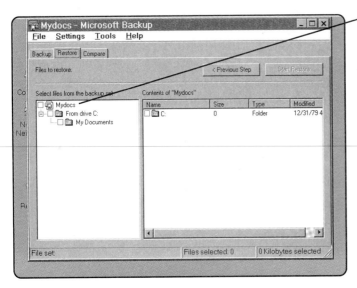

6. **Click twice on** the **name** of your backup file (in this example, Mydocs). The names of the files contained in the backup file will appear in the Contents box.

Notice both of the files that you backed up in this example are checked (✔). If you do not want to restore a specific file, you can click on it to *remove* the ✔.

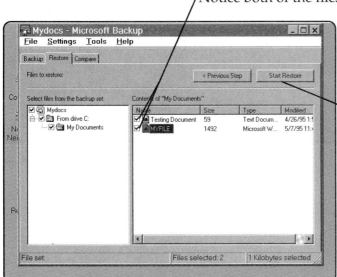

7. **Click** on **Start Restore**. The Restore dialog box will appear.

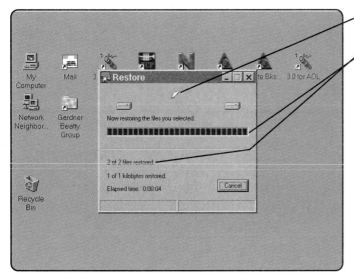

Notice the flying image.

Notice that this dialog box keeps you informed of the restoration process.

Eventually, a Microsoft Backup dialog box will appear.

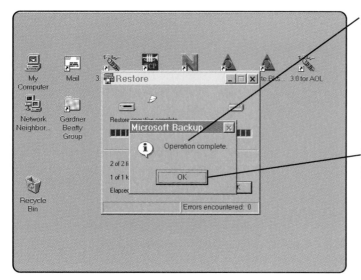

All restored!

Closing the Restore Program

1. Click on **OK**. The dialog box will close.

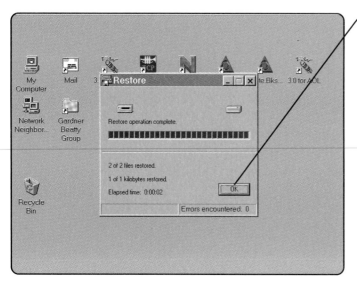

2. Click on **OK**. The Untitled Microsoft Backup dialog box will reappear.

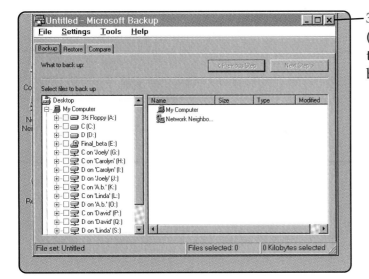

3. **Click** on the **Close button** ([X]) in the right corner of the title bar to close the dialog box.

RECAPPING

✔ The backup program will back up your entire system or selected files to floppy disks or a tape drive or an optical drive.

✔ You can back up a single file, multiple files from a specific folder, or a combination of files and folders. Your choice.

✔ Restoring files couldn't be easier. However, do be cautious about restoring files. You could accidentally write over a newer file with an older file .

Tuning Your Hard Drive

A hard drive is somewhat like your car's engine. If you take care of it and keep it tuned, it will give you great service for a long time. Windows 95 comes with two built-in hard drive maintenance programs. One is called ScanDisk. It checks for and fixes errors found on your hard drive. These errors have to do with how files are organized and relate to one another. The other program, called Defragmenter, consolidates files so that your computer can access individual files faster. In this chapter, you will do the following:

✔ Check for errors on your hard drive by using the ScanDisk program

✔ Consolidate your files by using the Defragmenter program.

CHECKING YOUR HARD DRIVE FOR ERRORS

Electronic files are sensitive creatures and can often become unusable or disorganized in such a way that your computer makes mistakes. The ScanDisk program searches for all different kinds of file errors and corrects them for you.

1. **Click twice** on the **My Computer icon**. The My Computer dialog box will appear, as shown here.

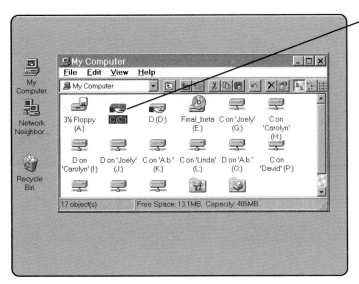

2. Move the mouse arrow to the **drive** you want **to scan** for errors. In this example, it is drive C.

3. Click the **right mouse button**. A menu will appear.

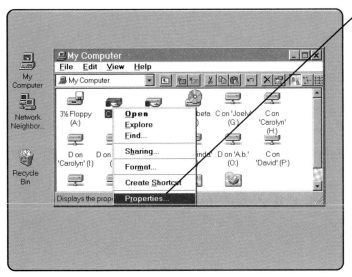

4. Click on **Properties**. The Properties dialog box will appear.

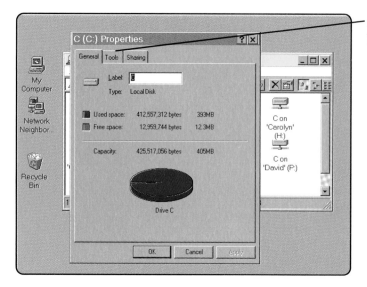

5. **Click** on the **Tools tab** to bring it to the front.

Checking Error Status

Notice that Windows keeps track of the last time you checked your hard drive for errors.

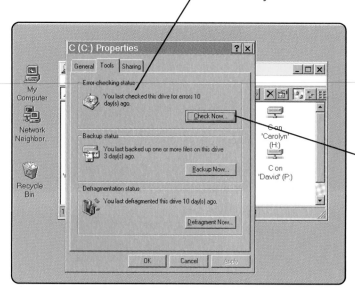

Selecting the Drive to Scan and the Scan Options

1. **Click** on **Check Now**. The ScanDisk - C(C:) dialog box will appear.

2. Click on **(C:)** to highlight it. (You can click on another drive later, if you want. ScanDisk scans only one drive at a time.)

We recommend that you use the standard error check about once a week, and more often if you use your computer for extended periods of time. Make sure that there is a dot in the circle here. If not, click on it to put a dot in the circle.

We do the Thorough scan about once a month. It takes a while, so pick a time when you can let your computer do its thing. To do a Thorough scan, you simply click here to put a dot in the circle.

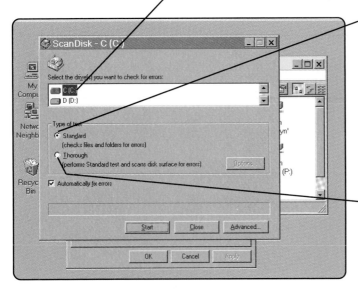

3. Click on **Automatically fix errors** to put a ✔ in the box if it is not already there.

Scanning for Errors

1. Click on **Start**. The scanning process will begin.

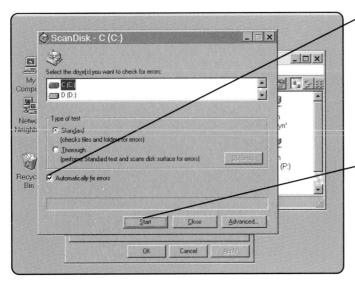

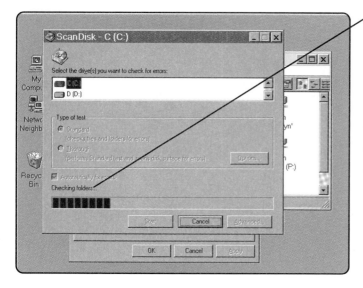

ScanDisk goes through its paces, checking folders and files for problems. When it finds problems, it fixes them automatically.

When it has completed its tasks, the ScanDisk Results dialog box will appear.

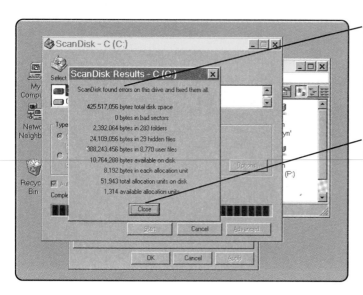

Notice all the current information about your hard drive, including the fact that ScanDisk found errors and fixed them!

2. **Click** on **Close**. All done. The dialog box will close.

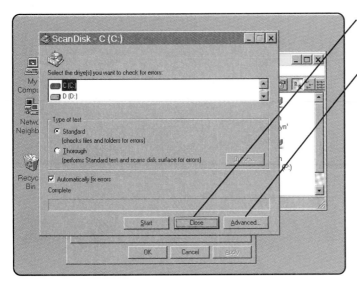

3. **Click** on **Close**. The dialog box will appear.

Notice the Advanced button. If you consider yourself a sophisticated user, you can click on this button and choose various options for the way ScanDisk handles errors. If not, stick with the standard ScanDisk process.

CONSOLIDATING YOUR FILES

Over time, as you open and close files, the files become fragmented. Parts of each file eventually get scattered all over the disk drive. This means that the computer has to search for the parts of a specific file before it can open it, slowing down the process. The Defragmenter program finds all the scattered parts and puts each file back together again. After that's done, your files will open faster!

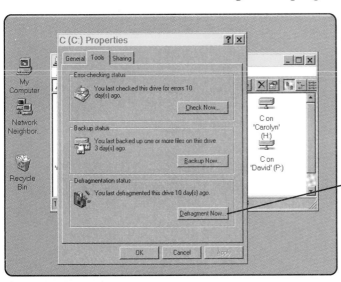

1. **Repeat steps 1 through 4** in the first section of this chapter to open this dialog box if it is not already open.

2. **Click** on **Defragment Now**. The Defragmenting Drive C dialog box will appear.

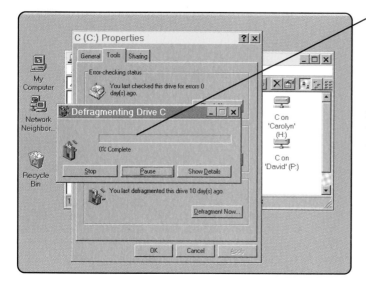

Notice that the Defragmenter program keeps you informed of its progress.

Note A: If your disk doesn't need to be defragmented, the Disk Defragmenter dialog box below will appear.

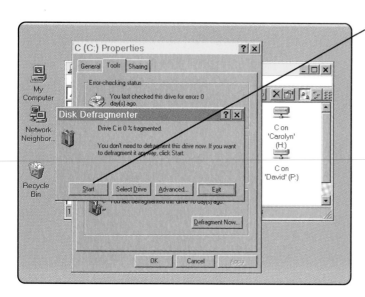

Note B: You can go ahead and defragment your drive anyway by clicking on Start. In this example, we did just that. The Defragmenting Drive C dialog box will appear.

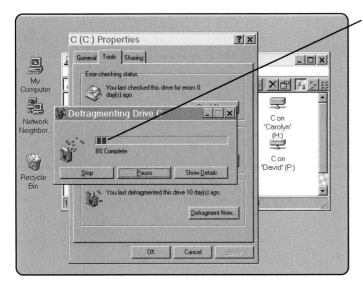

This is a slow process, so be patient. Perhaps you can go get a cup of tea and come back in 10 or 15 minutes.

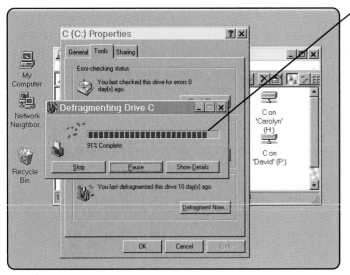

Back so soon? Well, we're almost done. However, the last 10 percent of the process is *very* slow.

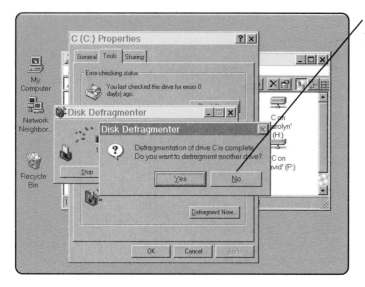

3. Click on **No**. The dialog box will close.

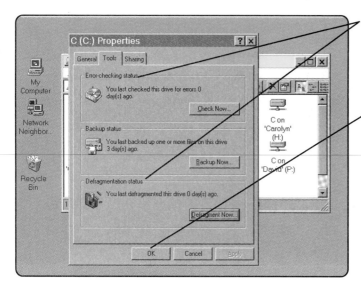

Notice that your status messages on error-checking and defragmentation are up-to-date!

4. Click on **OK**. The dialog box will close.

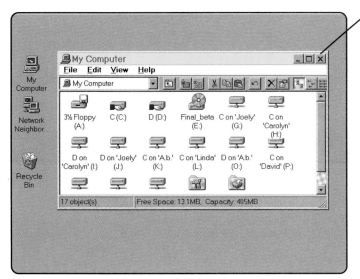

5. **Click** on the **Close button** ([×]) in the right corner of the title bar to close the window. Your hard drive is ready for warp speed!

RECAPPING

✔ Electronic files are sensitive creatures. Often, and for no apparent reason, they become corrupted, stubborn, disorganized, or dislocated. You may not even be aware of a problem until you get a strange error message. Therefore, it's a good idea to check for errors often and to let ScanDisk fix them.

✔ The more you open and close files, the more they become scattered or fragmented. This slows down your computer. Fortunately, you can consolidate your scattered files easily with Window's Defragmenter program. It's a good idea to check once a week to see if you need to run the Defragmentation program.

Making 95 Look Like 3.1

If you have lots of experience working in Windows 3.1, you may find it very frustrating to adjust to some aspects of Windows 95. At first we didn't like Windows 95, but, after struggling with its new challenges, we feel that it is worth the effort. One way to ease the frustration is to find ways to make Windows 95 work somewhat like Windows 3.1. In this chapter, you will do the following:

✔ Set up Windows 95 to run Program Manager

✔ Set up your Windows 95 desktop to have the look and feel of Windows 3.1

USING PROGRAM MANAGER

If you have upgraded from Windows 3.1, Program Manager is still resident on your hard drive. It is sleeping in the background, just waiting for its fans to reactivate it. It couldn't be easier.

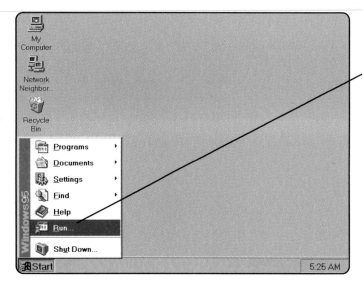

1. **Click** on **Start**. A menu will appear.

2. **Click** on **Run**. The Run dialog box will appear.

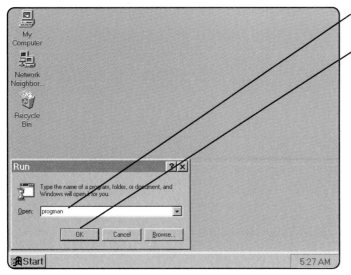

3. **Type progman**.

4. **Click** on **OK**. The Program Manager window will appear.

Well, there you are, the familiar Program Manager!

Believe it or not, these used to be your Windows 3.1 group icons. You will notice there are some group icons you didn't have in Windows 3.1. That's because Windows 95 created them.

Opening a Group Window

You can open one of your old Windows 3.1 group windows and, lo and behold, things will look almost the same as they used to. Your screen will look different if you had your group windows open when you upgraded.

1. **Click twice** on a **group icon**. The window will open.

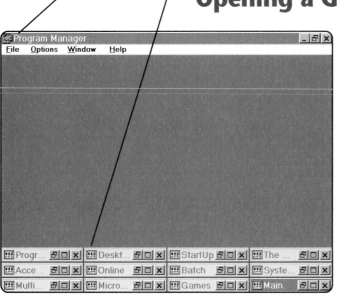

Look familiar? You can work the old way (this is what our desktop used to look like), but there is a price.

Working with Program Manager is slower, and you do not have ready access to the new features of Windows 95.

2. Click on the **Close button** (⊠) in the right corner of the Program Manager title bar to close Program Manager.

CREATING A NEW GROUP WINDOW FOR YOUR DESKTOP

You can create a folder icon that will open into a window right on your desktop. You can place shortcut icons for your favorite programs in it. It will open and function much like a group icon or window did in Windows 3.1.

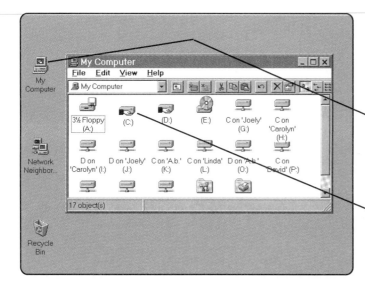

1. Click twice on **My Computer**. The My Computer window will appear.

2. Click twice on **(C:)**. The (C:) window will appear.

3. Click on **File** in the menu bar. A menu will appear.

4. Move the mouse arrow to **New**. Another menu will appear.

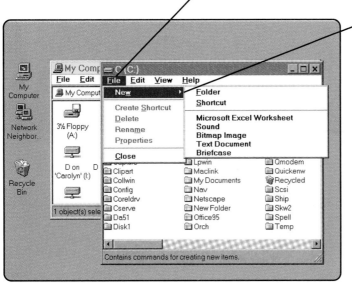

5. Click on **Folder**. A "New Folder" will appear in the window.

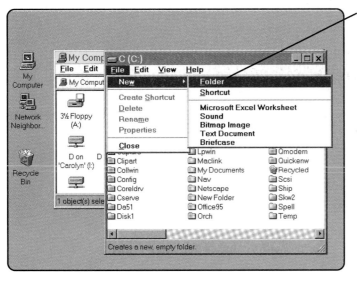

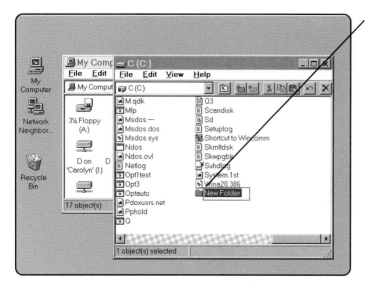

Notice that the newly created folder is highlighted and ready to be named.

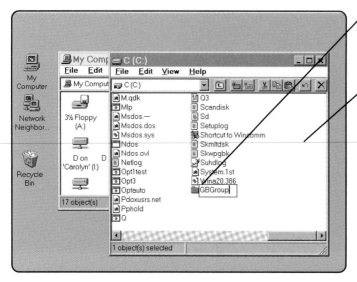

6. **Type** a **name** for the folder. In this example, we typed GBGroup.

7. **Click anywhere** on the white surface in the window to close the naming box. The folder is now labeled GBGroup.

MOVING THE FOLDER TO THE DESKTOP

In this section, you will move the newly created folder to the desktop. If this seems like déjà vu, it is. You moved a folder to the desktop in Chapter 10. The difference is that this folder is *empty* and contains no programs.

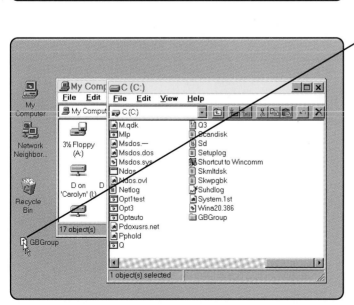

1. **Move** the mouse arrow to the **new** folder icon. In this example, it is the GBGroup folder.

2. **Press and hold** the **mouse button** and **drag** the **new folder icon** to the desktop. You may see a symbol, such as a plus sign (+) or a circle, attached to the arrow as you drag.

3. **Release** the mouse button. The folder icon will now appear on the desktop.

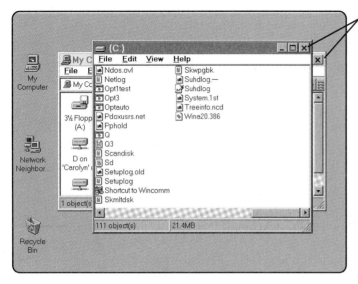

4. Click on the **Close buttons** (⊠) in the right corners of the title bars to close the windows.

MAKING THE DESKTOP LOOK LIKE WINDOWS 3.1

To complete the Windows 3.1 look-a-like customization, you will need to add shortcut icons to the desktop, move the task bar to the top, and put icons in your newly created "group window."

Moving Shortcut Icons to the Desktop

1. Repeat steps 1 through 6 in Chapter 10, the section entitled "Putting a Program Shortcut on the Desktop" on page 82, to put icons for the programs you use often on the desktop. As you can see, we've done that.

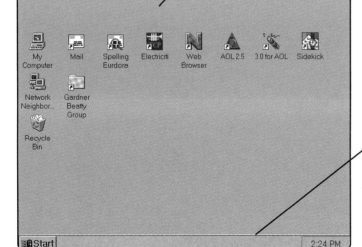

Relocating the Taskbar

1. Repeat steps 1 through 3 in the section entitled "Moving the Taksbar," in Chapter 10 to move the taskbar to the top of the desktop.

With the title bar at the top of the screen you will get a pull-down menu instead of a pop-up menu when you click on Start. We believe that this is more 3.1-like!

Putting Shortcut Icons into the "Group Icon"

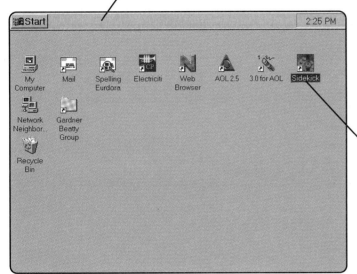

You can now put into your new "group window" the shortcut icons of programs you want to have ready access to but don't use as often as others.

1. Move the mouse arrow to the icon you want **to store** in your new group icon.

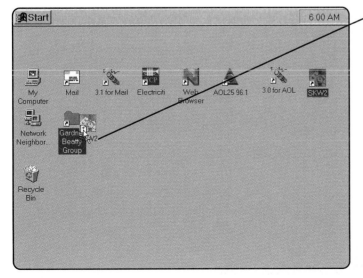

2. Press and hold the mouse button as you **drag** the **shortcut icon** to the folder icon (a plus sign (+) will appear attached to the arrow).

3. Release the mouse button. The shortcut icon will disappear into the folder icon.

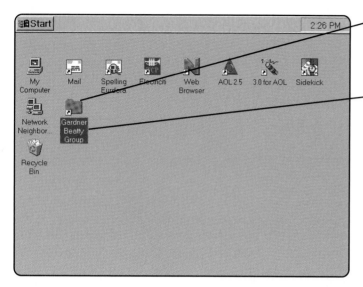

4. **Repeat steps 1 through 3** above to move other shortcut icons into the folder icon

5. **Click twice** on the **folder icon**. In this example, it is the GBGroup folder icon. The GBGroup window will appear.

RECAPPING

✔ You can run Program Manager in Windows 95, but we do not recommend that you work that way.

✔ You can customize the Windows 95 desktop to be more like a customized Windows 3.1 desktop. This one has the following features:

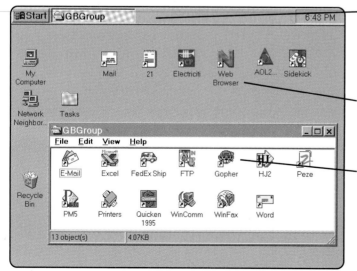

❶ The taskbar is on the top of the screen. This gives it a familiar "pull-down" menu when you click on Start.

❷ Our most-used program icons are on our desktop, ready to launch.

❸ The folder icon on our desktop acts like a Windows 3.1 group icon. It contains icons for programs that we launch several times a week.

WINDOWS 95

Part VI: Appendix

| Appendix: | Installing Windows 95 As an Upgrade | Page 256 |

Installing Windows 95 As an Upgrade

If you bought a brand new computer, Windows 95 may already be installed on it. But if you are upgrading from a previous version of Windows, this appendix will help. In this example, installation was done using a CD-ROM drive. Installing from floppy disks is the same as the CD installation shown here, but it's a little slower because it requires inserting and removing approximately 15 disks. In this appendix, you will do the following:

✔ Install Windows 95 as an upgrade to a previous version of Windows

UPGRADING TO WINDOWS 95

Each installation is different. The screens you will see will depend on your computer's software and hardware. Don't get nervous if your installation is slightly different from the one described here.

Getting Ready to Install

1. **Turn off** your **screen saver** and **close all programs** except Program Manager. Have a blank, formatted 3.5" high-density disk ready.

Installing

1. **Insert** the **Windows 95 CD** in your **CD-ROM** slot.

2. **Click** on **File** in the menu bar. The File menu will appear.

3. **Click** on **Run**. The Run dialog box will appear.

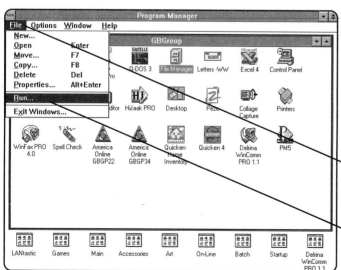

4. Type d:\win95\setup.exe (**Note:** If you have two hard drives, chances are that your CD-ROM drive will be called e:. In that case, type **e:\win95\setup.exe**

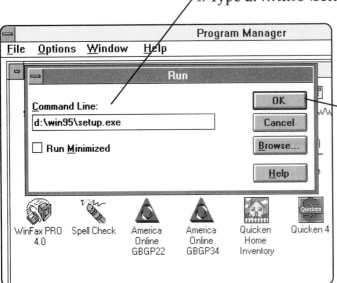

5. Click on **OK**. A Windows 95 Setup dialog box will appear.

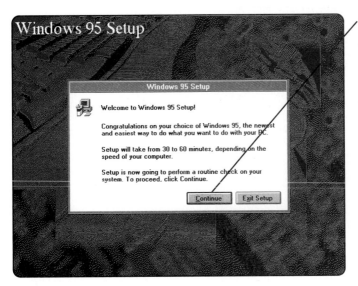

6. Click on **Continue**. Another Windows 95 Setup dialog box will appear.

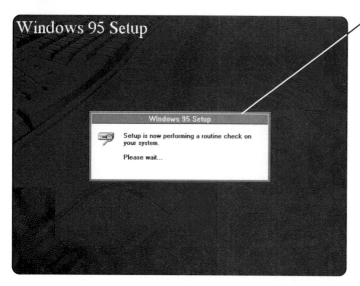

There will now be a fairly lengthy intermission while Windows performs its routine check.

Don't be surprised when the screen goes black for a moment. It's okay. After blackness, the Windows 95 Setup dialog box will appear.

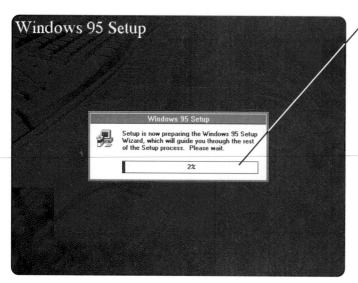

There will now be another fairly lengthy intermission while Windows gets its Setup Wizard installed. You will be informed of the progress here.

Next, the Windows 95 Setup Wizard dialog box will appear.

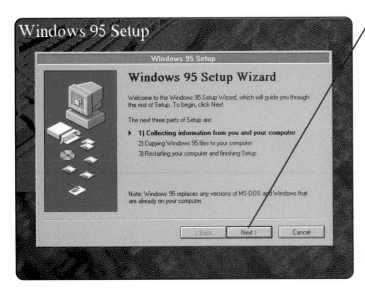

7. Click on **Next**. The Windows Setup Wizard (Choose Directory) dialog box will appear.

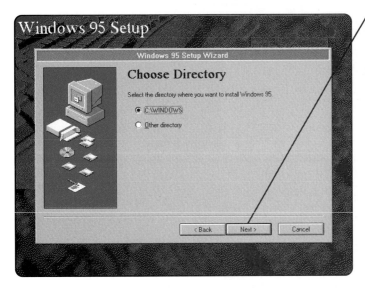

8. Click on **Next**. The Windows Setup Wizard (Preparing Directory) dialog box will appear.

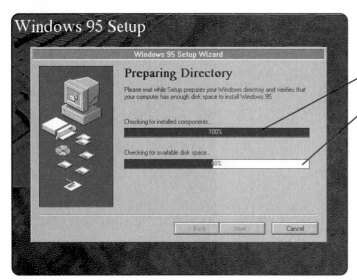

This process will take a while:

This bar will fill in first.

Next, this bar will appear and fill in. When it is filled in, the Windows 95 Setup Wizard (Save System Files) dialog box will appear.

Saving System Files

Windows 95 gives you the option of saving your old Windows and DOS files in case you need to uninstall Windows 95 for any reason. You will need space on your hard drive for both the old files and the new ones. If you have the space, we recommend that you choose "Yes" and do this. The old files can be deleted safely and easily after you're sure that Windows 95 is working properly with your computer. If you do not have the space, choose No and go on to the next section.

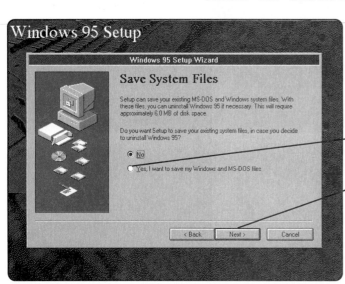

1. **Click** on **Yes** to place a dot in the circle.

2. **Click** on **Next**. The screen at the top of the next page will appear.

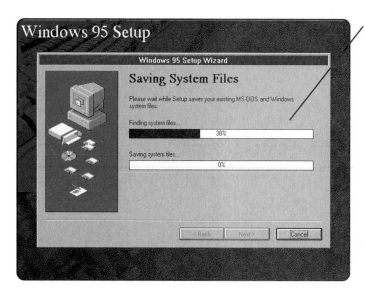

Setup locates the old Windows and DOS system files on your computer's hard disk.

After locating the files, Setup asks you where you want them backed up. Keep in mind that you will need about 30 megabytes of space on your C: drive to install Windows 95 over Windows 3.1.

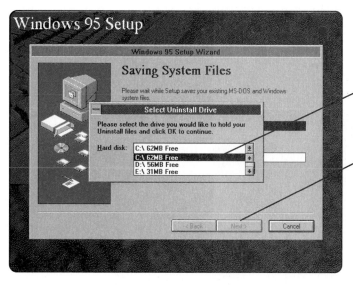

3. Click on the **drive** you want to use to back up your old system files.

4. Click on **Next**. Saving your old system files will take a few minutes. After this is done, the Windows 95 Setup Wizard (Setup Options) dialog box will appear.

Choosing the Setup Option

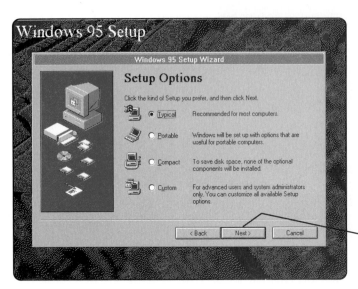

We recommend that you stick with the Typical installation. You can always add components later, when you become more familiar with Windows 95. See Chapter 20, the section entitled "Installing the Backup Program" for an example of how to install additional or missing components.

1. Click on **Next**. The Windows 95 Setup Wizard (User Information) dialog box will appear.

Identifying Yourself

On some of the installations we did, Windows filled in this area. In other cases, it did not. If your name and company are not filled in here, follow these steps:

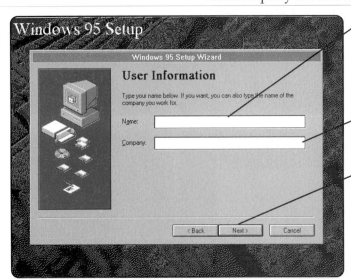

1. Type your **name** and **press** the **Tab key**. The cursor will move to the Company text box.

2. Type your **company name** (optional).

3. Click on **Next**. The Windows 95 Setup Wizard (Analyzing Your Computer) dialog box will appear.

Confirming Hardware

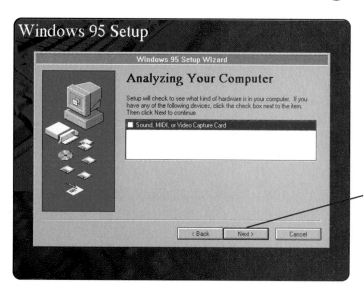

If Windows is not sure that you have a particular item, like the sound card shown here, you can click on the ☐ to put an X in it to confirm that your computer has it. Otherwise, go to the next step.

1. Click on **Next**. Another Windows 95 Setup Wizard (Analyzing Your Computer) dialog box will appear.

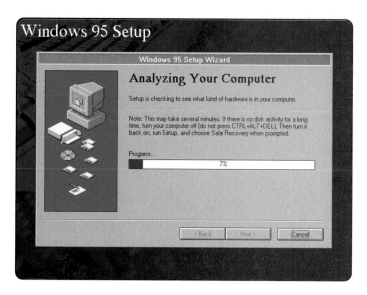

This process moves along rather smartly until it gets to about 81 percent when it starts to slow down. At 96 percent to 100 percent the process is like molasses (at least on the 12 installations we did). So hang in there! When the process is complete, another Windows 95 Setup Wizard (Get Connected) dialog box will appear.

Getting Connected

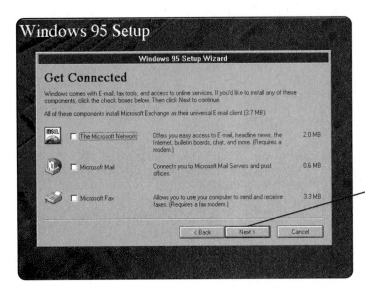

If you want to install one of these options, click on it to place an X in the square next to it. You can add any or all of these options later.

1. Click on **any option** you want to install.

2. Click on **Next**. Another Windows 95 Setup Wizard (Windows Components) dialog box will appear.

Selecting Components to Install

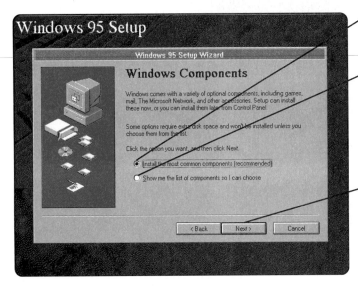

The recommended option is the safest way to go.

If you are an advanced Windows maven, you can click here to put a dot in the circle, then go on to the step below.

1. Click on **Next**. Another Windows 95 Setup Wizard (Startup Disk) dialog box will appear.

Making a Startup Disk

Here's where you will use that formatted, blank disk that we mentioned earlier. It is very important you make a startup disk, just in case something goes wrong. Computers and software are often unpredictable, and this disk could be a lifesaver!

1. Insert a blank, formatted **disk** in **drive A**.

2. Click on **Next**. A Windows 95 Setup Wizard (Start Copying Files) dialog box will appear.

3. Click on **Next**. A message, "Preparing to Copy Files," will appear briefly, followed by the appearance of another dark Windows 95 Setup dialog box.

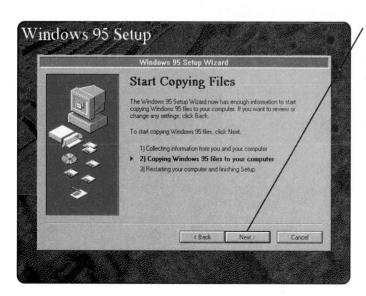

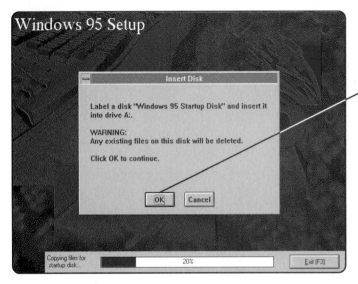

If you haven't already done so in step 1, insert a blank, formatted disk in drive A.

4. Click on **OK**. The copying proceeds.

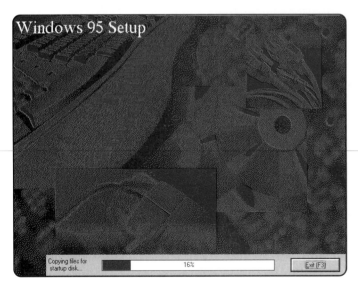

Copying continues. When the copying is complete, another Windows 95 Setup Disk dialog box will appear.

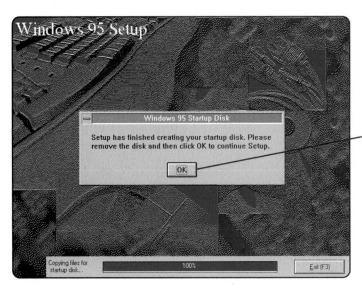

5. Remove the **disk** from drive A. If you have not already done so, put a label on the disk and store it in a safe place.

6. Click on **OK**. A Windows 95 Setup (Welcome) dialog box will appear.

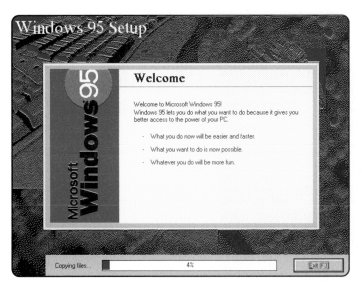

Copying continues. Eventually, another Windows 95 Setup Wizard (Finishing Setup) dialog box will appear.

RESTARTING YOUR COMPUTER TO FINISH THE INSTALLATION

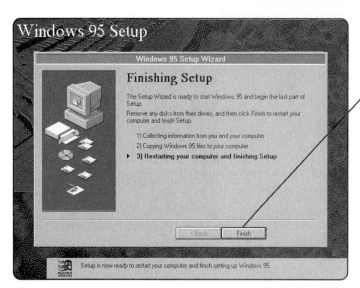

To complete the installation, you will have to restart your computer.

1. Click on **Finish**. In a moment or so, a message will appear at the bottom of your screen: "Getting Ready to Run Windows 95 for the First Time."

Getting Ready to Run Windows for the First Time ·

Watching, Watching

Be patient. This could take awhile.

Notice the message.

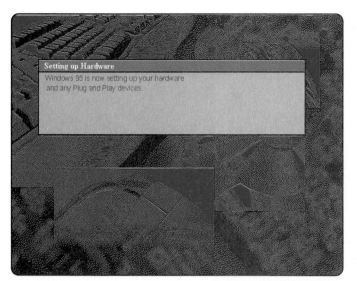

More Watching and Waiting

Screens like these will just come and go as Windows does its thing.

Hardware will be installed while you wait.

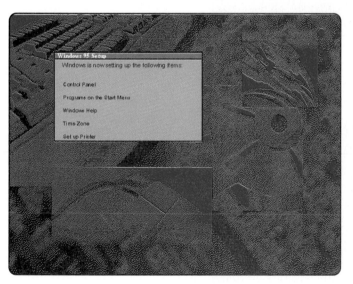

The Control Panel, items on the Programs menu, the Windows Help, and the Time Zone will be set up while you watch. If you did not have a printer installed previously, it will be installed.

SELECTING THE TIME ZONE

Windows already knows the time. What it needs for you to do is to tell it where you live so that your time zone can be recorded.

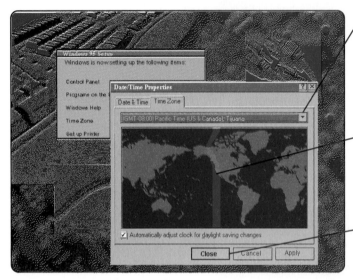

1. **Click** on the ▼ if you want to look at a list of time zones, and then click on your time zone.

OR

2. **Click** on the **area** where you live. Since we live in California, we chose it as the example.

3. **Click** on **Close**. A message box will appear

Eventually this message box will close and a Welcome to Windows dialog box, along with some desktop icons, will appear.

Depending on your computer's hardware, you may be asked to restart your computer again at this point.

SHUTTING DOWN

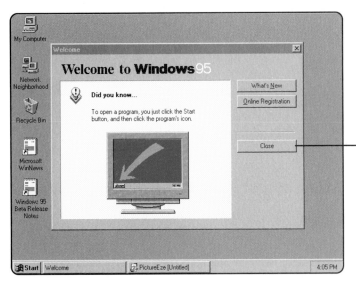

At this point, it's a good idea to shut down, turn your computer off, and then turn it back on to reboot it one more time, just to make sure that everything works.

1. **Click** on **Close**. The Welcome Dialog box will close.

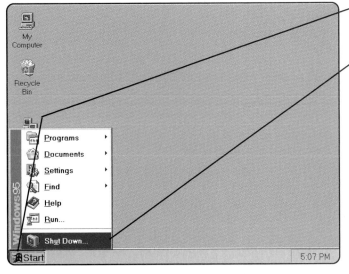

2. **Click** on **Start**. A pop-up menu will appear.

3. **Click** on **Shut Down**. The Shut Down Windows dialog box will appear.

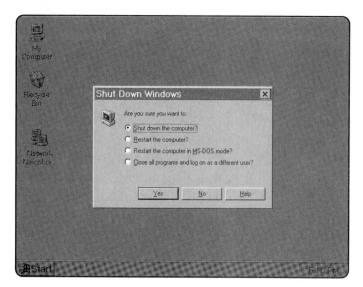

4. **Click** on **Yes**. Windows will close eventually. When a screen arrives that says you can turn off your computer (not shown here), please do so. Do not turn off your computer until the message appears.

RECAPPING

✔ You are now ready to jump into this new and exciting way to compute. Go to Chapter 1 and start your computer.

✔ You can register on-line by clicking on the Online Registration button that will appear on the Welcome screen the next time you boot up. Just follow along with the registration instructions. We prefer to register by mail and keep a photocopy in our files. It's up to you.

Index